CONTENTS

DEDICATION

To Dameon Brown Sr.,

the man I love.

ELISHA D. BROWN

JOURNAL *of* MIRACLES

DELIVERANCE AND HEALING
IN THE COVID-19 YEAR

ENDORSEMENTS

"THIS BOOK RESONATES WITH the miracle-working power of God to transform lives, and it all starts with a yielded heart. Though gifted in many ways, academically and musically, Elisha saw a disparity between the miracles that Jesus said His followers were to do, and what she was experiencing in life. So, believing in the God of miracles, she decided to do something about it! This book is testament to what can happen to the one who has the courage to take the road less traveled and believe in God's Word. Getting to know Elisha through our Spirit Lifestyle training has been a delight as she has grown and excelled in the things of the Spirit, especially healing miracles. There is no doubt that Elisha is part of a new generation of believers who are taking hold of God's promises and running with them, 'laying hold of that for which Christ Jesus took hold of me' and living out the greater works in our time. This book will inspire and encourage you to be one of those, like Elisha, who takes God at His word and steps out in faith to demonstrate the love and power of Jesus today."

Rob and Aliss Cresswell,
Authors and Founders of SpiritLifestyle.com and Miracle Cafés

"Elisha's book chronicles a journey in the love of God for His creation. She has tapped into a maturity and intimacy in Him that flows to the reader in faith building chapters as expectation and hope rises in the hearts of the reader to a level of inspiration to seek the one true God that is glorified in her testimonies. It is an honor to write about such a devoted and selfless woman of God. She exemplifies the character of Christ as she seeks daily to live for Him. She truly rules and reigns with the authenticity and power of the Holy Spirit as she gives her all in the service of others and her family. Her joy is truly in the strength of the Lord and her passion seated firmly at His right hand to defeat the works of the enemy, set the captives free and mend the hearts of the broken hearted. Her belief truly moves mountains and makes the path straight for the Dunamis power of our King to be displayed to the world. She is a warrior for the justice and righteousness of God to invade earth as in Heaven. Her humility is a lesson of divine obedience to us all...A MUST READ!"

L. Mark Yow
Founder of 13th of Grace Apostolic Ministry

"God has truly inspired Elisha to write this Journal of Miracles!! I am so moved by the many testimonies, and I declare that millions will catch on to faith and receive their miracles upon reading this literary piece. This is a must read for the masses, especially for those in need of a miracle."

Mother Vanessa Slack
New Christ Temple COGIC

INTRODUCTION

Life is a miracle. So many amazing things can happen unexpectedly in a lifetime. I want to testify of my personal experiences and adventures as a wife, mother, Christian minister, and Spirit Lifestyle coach. These are my passions; I dedicate my life to serve God in each of these capacities. I'm also an electrical engineer and do freelance modeling for local agencies where I'm hired for commercial, runway, print, and billboard advertisements. With God helping me, I've chosen to take my everyday life and place it at His feet. Inquiring of Him concerning everything. I believe because of that mindset, certain supernatural things started to happen in my life. I've embraced God's process, and He's given my life new meaning.

I've always been drawn to God, even as a little kid. I would take every single doll I had, dress them in their best, and create a church for us. I had so many dolls that I could only pull this off in the basement of the home I grew up in, the Berkshire house in Detroit, Michigan. My doll church consisted of a plushy blanket strategically folded in an oblong shape to accommodate our seating. I would sit every doll in calculated rows, I would sing a song, talk to God, and then wait for Him. I got discouraged at times when I made appointments with God to meet me in my room. I would clean thoroughly, keep watch on the clock, then pop my head in while slowly opening the door asking, "God, are you here?" The dolls and I were dressed and ready on several occasions for the rapture of the church. I'm tickled as I think of the drive and consistency as I waited and continued to prepare. This carried on throughout my elementary and middle school years. I loved God then and even more so now. I'm so glad He covered me. Now that I'm older, I understand that parts of what I've grown to be were present even in the little girl I used to be.

I've grown to love prayer after I had an encounter with the Holy Spirit when I was twenty years old. This intrigued me and lit a fire of desire to study the spiritual implications that take place in prayer. That same year, I had my encounter with the Holy Spirit, and my husband and I started our journey together serving in Christian ministry. We've served in different capacities of the local church over the years and then started a family ministry called Righteous Antidote in 2012. That was around the same time I also connected with a ministry in the United Kingdom called Spirit Lifestyle with Rob and Aliss Cresswell. I officially partnered with them and became a coach alongside many others in different parts of the world in 2020—the year of COVID-19. A Spirit Lifestyle coach is devoted to helping transform the lives of people by directing them to Jesus, teaching them to live a life led by the Holy Spirit, and extending His Kingdom in love and power to others as they move forward in their journey. As I began to coach, many miracles occurred, and I was encouraged to document them. I've seen miracles before, but not on a weekly basis like this. I don't attempt to pretend that I have all the answers. I just see God keeping His Word. The Word of God is unchanging. Isaiah 55:11 says, "*So shall My word be that goes forth from My mouth; It shall not return to Me void, but it shall accomplish what I please, and it shall prosper in the thing for which I sent it.*" Jesus is the word and Jesus has returned to the Father. Psalms 107:20 says, "*He sent His word and healed them, and delivered them from their destructions.*" What it says today it will say hundreds of years from now. I can only share what I've seen as I've believed; many were healed and delivered. Some are still contending for complete wholeness through Jesus. This book shares some of my experiences and learnings.

Year 2020, the start of COVID-19 was one of the toughest years for all of us. Many in our world suffered due to the pandemic. It can be considered boastful and inconsiderate to some to share the amazing things that I saw and are still happening to this day. Nonetheless, I was arrested by the Holy Spirit, and He placed in my heart, "Tell them what you've experienced on this journey."

I will be honest: I was afraid to start coaching. This is nothing I would ever jump to do. I've always been the person who would serve in ministry in the background. I was comfortable with that. I would sing in the choir but to sing a solo or to be a speaker would always be a challenge for me. My hands would sweat, and my heart would start pounding in my chest. When my husband started our family ministry, Righteous Antidote, I would do the work in the background and intercede for him as the voice and representative. He would teach, preach, produce, and write music. I would just look on with amazement at the gifts that God placed in Him. I thought to myself, *surely my only calling is to be an intercessor for Him and our children.*

I didn't know how powerful intercession could be, but the more I spent time in prayer, the more my eyes were opened. For over a decade, my experiences would be to sit quietly in my prayer closet, praying and listening to the Holy Spirit, writing songs, and interceding for all who would drop in my mind. Praying seemed better suited for me than anything else because it was just me and God. I was shy, quiet, plain, unassuming, never seeking attention, very introverted. By the time our daughter was born in 2005, I was finishing my requirements at Wayne State University. I earned a master's degree in electrical engineering. God placed in me a craving to solve problems. It was somewhat fulfilled in engineering, but something was still missing. Whilst being an undergraduate, my little daughter would play throughout the house and run into my closet, where she would find me sitting on the floor with my Bible in front of me. I enjoyed praying the scriptures because I always wanted to pray but didn't always know what to pray. At times I would just get lost in His presence and didn't need words. I would have these moments where I felt time would stop. I visualized laying in God's arms with my ear against His chest. Listening to the beat of His heart, seeking to operate from His rhythm. I would look up and realize with amazement that three hours had passed. God knew I would be a Christian minister today; I believe those prayer moments stirred up supernatural desire in me that I didn't know could exist. I wasn't fully satisfied in life until I obeyed Him by partnering with His Spirit, seeking to cultivate all the gifts He had placed in me. To stop running and being afraid. I've learned on my journey that true wholeness only comes through the Holy Spirit, walking in our divine destinies.

Jesus told us what would happen if we partnered with the Holy Spirit in John 16:7, "*Nevertheless I tell you the truth. It is to your advantage that I go away; for if I do not go away, the Helper will not come to you; but if I depart, I will send Him to you.*" We have the comforter through Jesus. If we yield to Him, our lives will be forever changed for the better. It does not matter our background or where we come from. Whether we are overlooked, unassuming, average, or considered unqualified by others. It is written in 1 Corinthians 1:27, "*But God has chosen the foolish things of the world to put to shame the wise, and God has chosen the weak things of the world to put to shame the things which are mighty*". My goal for sharing testimonies is to display the difference it makes. From just believing there is a God; to believing *in* God who is with us in the highs and lows in life. Also, that God can use anybody, even little me, to encourage, that we need to seek in building a relationship with God, having faith in Him and standing on His Word. So many believe that there is a God but think He's far away and uninterested. That couldn't be further from the truth. I pray that the experiences I share in this book will start wildfires for Jesus. Just like God did in the book of Acts, He gave us keys and examples in building the Kingdom of God.

I pray as you read this book that you will experience healings and miracles for your spirit, soul, and body. That you will be moved to draw even closer to God, to find your identity in Him, seeking a deeper relationship. That it will become normal for your intimate prayer times to spill out into all the world and touch everyone you encounter. That you will experience the splendor of the Holy Spirit and the unexplainable joy of being used by Him for the Kingdom. That your eyes will be opened to not only know that there is a God but to believe in Him for your breakthrough. To not be overwhelmed by crisis but to be overwhelmed by God and who He is. Graced to overcome oppression, traumas, sicknesses, or tragedy. That you will be comforted by the comforter from this day forth. Holy Spirit guiding you into all truth and victory in Jesus' name. Amen.

Chapter One

FIRST ENCOUNTERS WITH THE HOLY SPIRIT

"When I found the one I love. I held him and would not let him go." Song of Solomon 3:4

I first encountered the Holy Spirit at my grandfather's church, who was Pastor Lorris Upshaw Senior. I was born in 1980 and raised in my grandfather's church. He was my pastor for twenty years. My parents served under his ministry also. There would be an altar call on Sundays where Granddad would share on the importance of being ready, that if Jesus would come back for His church and we are found with sin, we would not make it to heaven. I would feel a strong tug in my heart every time—seriously, every time. I found myself on the altar many Sundays as a child. No one had to coerce me to go. I could not explain the conviction in my soul. I could not express in words the desire I had to know God and have a relationship with His Holy Spirit. I just knew that Jesus was the answer to all my desires. My grandfather was a man of distinction and honor. I knew he knew Jesus, and I wanted what he had. Sometimes I was the only one that went to the front of the church during the altar call. Many must have thought I was a troubled child, but God was planting seeds in my heart. I didn't care what people thought of me. I think others were embarrassed for me. I saw the looks and was even asked by people after church why I always went. I didn't have the words to explain it. I just wanted what I read about in the scriptures and couldn't comprehend that Jesus was right there already for us all.

I knew miracles and healings were happening around me, but I did not see them. I sat in the middle of the church, not really understanding all that was being taught, but the foundation of what I needed was planted in my heart. My parents brought my siblings and I to Sunday school and then we would head into prayer and worship. I don't know exactly when it happened, but over those years, my heart was touched, and my desire to know God was kindled. I'm not saying that this can only happen for people who are raised in a church. God can do the same for someone who starts a walk with Him later in life. This is just how it happened for me.

The older I got, the more I would talk to our heavenly Father. One Sunday as a teen, I remember looking up to the ceiling and talking to Him. I asked Him, "Where are you? There has to be more to what I am seeing." Although I did not recognize it then, I know now He heard me and had many things He would show me in time. I had to go through a process because I believed He existed but assumed He was far away and what could happen for me would be limited. Now I understand what Matthew 7:7 means: "Keep on asking, and you will receive what you ask for. Keep on seeking, and you will find. Keep on knocking, and the door will be opened to you."

One Sunday, my grandfather shared an experience that I will never forget. It really opened my eyes to some realities. I knew my granddad was human like the rest of us, but as a kid I thought of him as superhuman, never able to make a mistake. All I saw him doing is serving God, a distinguished leader. When we entered the church on Sunday mornings, he was on his knees praying already. He was always giving and preaching with authority. I can't tell you of the scriptures or the topics of his messages, but this one story for some reason I remember so vividly. He said he was traveling one day and saw a woman in a wheelchair. He continued his way as he was rushing to meet a deadline. A short time after he saw her, Jesus spoke to him clearly saying, "If you had only prayed for her, she would have been healed and got up." This shook him to his core. Hearing those words caused tears to leap from his eyes. He said he could do nothing but cry in that moment. He was forever changed and learned more about the heart of Jesus from that experience. He said he never let an opportunity pass by without offering prayer again. I know now that God purposely allowed me to hear my grandfather's testimony clearly that day. Now, whenever I see someone who's feeling poorly, or if someone shares with me how they are feeling, I remember my grandfather's experience. I offer prayer, whether it is rejected or not. I don't want to ever turn down an opportunity to share Jesus. So many amazing things transpired from my grandfather's ministry. He and my grandmother touched so many lives for Jesus, especially mine. Their examples and prayers are always in my heart. I am because of the seeds they've sown in me, for their transparency and light.

Lorris and Nellie Upshaw Sr. (My leaders, my grandparents, resting in heaven now.)

YEAR 2000

I married the love of my life in March of 2000 at twenty years old. We met at my grandfather's church. He and I started our journey together, but we also individually started a journey in search of a relationship with the Holy Spirit. All my life, I was taught that there is a God, but I grew to the point where I desired to know of Him. I wanted to know Him for myself; that was my goal. I heard my grandparents talk of Him, I heard my parents talk of Him, I read about Him, but oh, to know Him due to a personal experience—that would be amazing, right? I went on several fasts, prayed throughout the year, and asked God to turn the search light on me, to expose anything that would prevent me from having oneness with Him. To prevent anything Satan could use to cause a wedge to block me from being filled with the Holy Spirit. I specifically prayed that God would go into the cracks, into the hidden places of my heart. You know those hard-to-reach places when you're cleaning your house. God started to show me things I had to let go, like grudges and unforgiveness from experiences I endured up until that point. It was not easy, but I laid it at the feet of Jesus. Mark 11:25 reads, "*And whenever you stand praying, if you find that you carry something in your heart against another person, release him and forgive him so that your Father in heaven will also release you and forgive you of your fault.*" This was the key that closed the door that the enemy used to prevent me from truly connecting with the Holy Spirit.

Although I was attending my husband's church at the time, we would visit my grandfather's church frequently. On one of those visits, there was an altar call once the message was preached. I can't tell you why this time was different from other times—only God knows when we are ready. I walked up to the altar with lots of other people. We began to pray and close our eyes. I found myself focusing on the cross, like I drifted away and was in a world all by myself. It was as though everyone in the room disappeared. I remember lifting my hands and just crying out to God. For that moment, it was just God and me. No one touched me. We were all lifting our voices in worship in the church. The elders were walking through the crowd, touching and agreeing with the people in prayer. They probably would have eventually prayed for me, but they didn't get the opportunity to. Suddenly, as I stood on my own, I felt as though a weighted blanket of glory swooped down over me. It happened as quick as the blinking of an eye. Suddenly I could hardly stand. My footing was no longer stable, and I began to stagger. I realized that He was in the room, that I was having an encounter with the Holy Spirit whom I had been seeking. I truly feel that because I went on a journey to rid myself of all the garbage I'd been carrying, I could receive a touch from God. What amazed me and truly opened my eyes was that nobody had to touch me. He came as I surrendered all I was to Him.

HEALED FROM FOOD POISONING

That same year, not long after my Holy Spirit encounter at my grandfather's church, I had another amazing experience. My husband and I were the musical guests for a conference. I would sing and my husband would play the organ. Days heading up to the conference, I stopped by the local mall to pick up some items. While shopping, I grabbed some pretzels and dip from the concession stand to snack on.

By the time I was walking out of the mall, I noticed my stomach was not well at all. Later that day at a rehearsal for the conference, while in the presence of my husband and other singers, I blacked out for a moment because my stomach was so weak. It was determined that I had food poisoning from my snack at the mall. The cheese dip was expired. I could not eat or drink for days, which drained me of the little strength I had left. I felt terrible and juggled with the idea of staying home, but because I was on the program and expected to be there, I self-medicated and went to the conference. I sang my part and sat for the rest of the evening. The speaker for that night was Lady Jaqueline

Thomas. When she finished the message, she led us into worship. The atmosphere shifted, and I noticed many were crying out to God, some were on the floor unable to stand, some were dancing, some were shouting, some were running. The glory of our Lord entered the conference hall and those who did not know Him were introduced in a single moment.

I gathered strength to stand and wave my hands. I figured that's the least I could do in such a beautiful atmosphere. That's when it happened. My eyes were closed, but my husband caught a glimpse of what was occurring and told me about it later. The speaker spotted me across the room. She made her way toward me. Her eyes were fixed as though the Holy Spirit had revealed something to her. Maneuvering her way around those who were dancing, jumping, shouting, and on the floor, she was determined to reach me. All I remember is worshiping, joining in with this mighty sound that had filled the conference hall. Then I heard a lady's voice say firmly, "*I rebuke you, sickness!*" She touched my stomach, right in the area that was pained from not eating and the food poisoning attacking my digestive system. I immediately felt what seemed to be a ten-pound chain jerk from around my waist and stomach. It was so strong that it caused me to stagger forward. The pain wrapped all the way around my waist, but when she prayed for me, it yanked off as if to snap from the back and cascade through the front until it was no longer present. I did not know what was happening to me. I did not open my eyes to even see what was going on. I didn't have to look. I felt Him, my beloved Holy Spirit. It registered in my mind that there's no way she could have known that I had food poisoning. The Holy Spirit must have given her a word of knowledge.

While all this was happening, I lifted my hands to the high heavens and opened my mouth to show my gratitude to the Father. Lo and behold, a language gushed from my mouth as a running river—uninterrupted words that I had never heard before. For that moment, I did not think, I did not try to understand, and I had no control over it. I just surrendered, the river flooded on the inside as living water, but burned to the outside as fire. It came from my innermost being. It was the Act II experience that I had been seeking. Nothing else in the world mattered in that moment. I was overcome and aware of His indescribable nearness. I was healed, the pain completely left my body, and I was filled all in the same embrace with the evidence of tongues. A fire ignited in my belly, and once I realized what was happening, I did not want it to end. It was my beloved; He found me, and I did not want to let go.

I placed my hand over my mouth in shock. As soon as I put my hands down, the rushing of the Holy Spirit continued. I backed up against the wall, my heart racing, my body shaking, feeling no pain, feeling the best I've ever felt in my entire life. This was earth-shaking. I thought my first experience at my grandfather's church was how it would always be. No, there are levels to this. I was overwhelmed with His beauty.

I was completely undone, submerged, flooded with power that I never could have dreamed of. You would think after all the fasting and praying I did to deny my flesh that I would be prepared, that I would be calm and understanding. But there was nothing calm about it. I knew I was not worthy to receive this love, and I'm still astounded in knowing this is how close He wants to be with us all. This is how it was before the fall of man. I felt light, so excited and full of joy. I wanted to tell everyone I knew. After that conference, I tested my stomach out by eating a huge burger! It was as though I was never sick.

A healing and a filling! This was my day to receive more. I encourage everyone to go after God like this. If you have not had a personal experience with Him, don't stop seeking, knocking, and asking. Just be in expectation and open to any way He wants to touch you. Just a heads up: it is amazing and your mind is going to be blown. Over twenty years later, my experiences in the year 2000 have never left me, and I've had so many other moments with Him. It just gets sweeter and sweeter. I'm in love and intrigued with our heavenly Father, precious Jesus, and beloved Holy Spirit. He is with us.

STEPPING OUT IN FAITH

After my encounter with the Holy Spirit, I found myself reading more scriptures to investigate the power of God. It is written that when Jesus was filled, He was empowered to heal the sick, raise the dead, and cast out demons. Luke 4:14 says Jesus returned to Galilee, filled with the Holy Spirit's power. Luke 4:18-19 reads, "*The Spirit of the Lord is upon me, for he has anointed me to bring Good News to the poor. He has sent me to proclaim that captives will be released, that the blind will see, that the oppressed will be set free, and that the time of the Lord's favor has come.*" I was reading the New Testament and noticed that everywhere Jesus went, He healed ALL (Matthew 8:16). Jesus is God's will expressed in the earth. If God did not want us to be free—spirit, soul, and body—He would not have given us Jesus. So, this caused me to start thinking in a new way. The old order of things was demolished when Jesus came. God made it possible for us to be saved, healed, and delivered.

Isaiah 53:5 says, "*But He was wounded for our transgressions, He was bruised for our iniquities; The chastisement for our peace was upon Him, And by His stripes we are healed.*" Some only think that Jesus came to save our souls. But just like Jesus brought salvation for our souls, He brings healing for our bodies. He does a complete work in us when we believe in Him. We don't serve a partial Jesus; we have access to the whole inheritance. Psalms 103:2-3 says, "*Bless the Lord, O my soul, and forget not all His benefits: Who forgives all your iniquities, who heals all your diseases.*" Forgiving our iniquities indicates freedom from all our wrongdoing, which means deliverance spiritually and adoption into the family of our Lord. Healed from diseases indicates alleviation of external attacks in the physical body. According to these scriptures, by faith we can be healed spiritually and physically. It is as simple as confessing Jesus as our Lord and Savior (Romans 10:9-10).

I started to look for opportunities on my job and in my school to testify of Jesus. I wanted to share what happened to me and how God is more real than we sometimes think. He's always there and loves us so much. Even with the little understanding and nervousness I had, I was in expectation of more. I was convinced that there was work that I could do for His Kingdom. Like Romans 8:28 says, "*And we know that all things work together for good to those who love God, to those who are the called according to His purpose.*" Nothing on the earth could take the place of my desire to be one with the Father; this relationship is everything. There is a hunger down in my soul. I knew He was close and watching my every move. When challenges came, I turned to Him.

I didn't do everything right, but there was no doubt in my mind that if I laid everything at the feet of Jesus, He would make a way. That was my approach for myself and for those around me.

DAD HEALED FROM KIDNEY STONES

That same year (2000), I spoke to my dad (Lorris Upshaw Jr.), who was experiencing painful kidney stones at the time. Since my Holy Spirit experience, I noticed when I heard of my dad not feeling well, I had a strong urgency to stop by the house to pray with him. He was at work, and the pain hit him hard. His supervisor sent him home and was expecting it would take a few days before he would be returning to work. He went to the doctors immediately, and they confirmed the pain was from kidney stones. They gave him a prescription to fill, but it was delayed. So, he went home. The pain was too great for words. He could not eat anything; if he tried to eat, he would vomit it right up. As soon as I left work, I drove by to see him. I didn't know what would happen, but one thing I knew: our Jesus did not want him to be in pain. When I arrived, he told me more of the situation. The doctors told him that after the prescription is filled and he starts to take the medicine, it would take three days to work. The kidney stones would eventually pass through his system followed by a blood clot. The blood clot would mean the stones and pain was clear.

I asked him if I could go ahead and pray, and he said, "Of course." I got down on my knees in front of my dad and laid my hands on his stomach. I can't remember all of what I prayed, but it was something simple like, "Dear heavenly Father, we thank You for who You are. We thank You for being God all by Yourself. This here is Your servant, and we know that it is not Your desire for him to be in pain. We rebuke kidney stones and command them to leave this body now in the name of Jesus." Nothing seemed to happen in that moment, but we both agreed in that moment that it was in God's hands. I gave him hugs and kisses, and then headed home. He later told me that minutes after I left, interesting things started to happen. Within fifteen minutes' time, he was healed. The kidney stones passed, and then a blood clot passed. All the excruciating pain he was feeling stopped. Hallelujah! He never got the prescription filled. He never needed it.

He returned to work the next day looking refreshed as though nothing ever happened. His supervisor thought this was suspicious. My dad was approached and bombarded with questions. He tried to explain to the supervisor that he was miraculously healed, but that story sounded too good to be true. The supervisor ended up issuing him an employee disciplinary write-up for pretending to be sick just to get off work or something. But my dad didn't care. He was so happy and blown away at God, rejoicing to be pain-free. What was supposed to require medicine and three days to recover, God removed in a matter of minutes.

When I heard of this, I was completely awe-struck. To this day, whenever I experience healings and miracles, I am just as in awe as the person who was just healed. That's our beloved Holy Spirit. It's a shame that the supervisor could not receive this good news of what our God can do. That supervisor just could not see it. It is hard for some to believe something like this unless it happens to them. This is the normal Christian life. To experience healing and deliverance always. If we shut God out, we won't be able to see the mighty works of His hands. Jesus explained in Matthew 13:14, "*This fulfills the prophecy of Isaiah that says, when you hear what I say, you will not understand. When you see what I do, you will not comprehend.*" I'm praying that more people will be like Matthew 13:16: "*But blessed are your eyes, because they see; and your ears, because they hear.*"

My dad, Pastor Lorris Upshaw Jr., and I

RISING EARLIER TO PRAY

Years went by, and I focused a lot of my energy in studying and finishing up at the University (WSU). During that time, God blessed my husband and I with three beautiful children. We all grew together doing ministry in different ways, namely praying together and studying the Bible. We had our hands full as parents, but we just kept lifting one another before the Lord. Life started to get busy as you can imagine. Working full-time and trying to keep up with our kids' schedules was tough. Some days, I would take the modeling jobs; other days I would be back to electrical engineering. Then we would have the scheduled dentist or primary care appointment for the kids when necessary. My husband travels a lot doing Righteous Antidote music ministry. Sometimes it was just the kids and me. When he traveled, I felt like the Uber driver, dropping the kids off to school and running to pick them up at their different locations as soon as I was off work. Then there's homework and cooking when I got home. Weekends flooded with laundry and cleaning house. I kept reminding myself that my family was my first ministry and that it would not always be so busy. That didn't mean I didn't miss spending hours in the prayer closet like I did before our family grew.

I asked God how I could incorporate more prayer and just time for Him and me. He spoke to my heart to rise early before anyone else and meet with Him, so that I did. I cleared an area in my closet and set my alarm to 3:00 a.m., 4:00 a.m. if I'm extremely sleepy or pressed snooze too many times. Then I would spend time talking to God about all things and certain people He would place on my heart to intercede for. This schedule seemed to work back then and still does today. Before having to wake the kids, get breakfast ready, making sure everyone is washed and dressed, praying with them, and dropping them off to school, I have quiet time with the Father. I would encourage all of us with kids to be open and transparent in our walk with God to our children. As mine have grown older, during breakfast it is common for everyone to read their Bibles and get the living bread in them also. It's normal for us to have biblical conversations and share the yearnings in my heart to please Jesus. They see the importance of sitting at His feet, not getting so busy with everything else that we give Him no time.

I told them the differences between Mary and Martha. How I was so busy when they were smaller that I felt like Martha, just always busy doing work, but God showed me how I can be like Mary, found sitting at the feet of Jesus (Luke 10:39). Mary was soaking up all Jesus would say and learning of His ways. Learning all about Jesus and the Holy Spirit positioned me to develop a deeper and more intimate relationship with my Creator. It helped me to keep my sanity when everything felt out of control around me.

SURPRISE MIRACLE AT THE PARK
SATURDAY, MAY 24, 2014

Knowing who we are in God, knowing who Jesus is to us, that we have access to living water, that we have all authority to pull down mountains and cast them into the sea—this is the best news I could have ever learned on my journey. The best thing I could have ever done is step out in faith to see Him work.

One hot day, my family went to a park called "George, George." My husband had been limping because his ankle was tender; it started a few months prior. We thought maybe it started from wearing shoes without good support. But the tenderness did not go away even when the shoes were replaced. I thought maybe with all the traveling he'd been doing, he just needed to rest it, but it didn't seem to want to go away. That day in the park, our kids were running about at play and my husband went after them so they would not go too far off. The boys were only five years and three years old then. It seemed whenever we went to the park, they would take off running. My husband did not see clearly as he was chasing after them, including a large branch through the grass in front of him. As he attempted to catch up after the kids, he stepped on that branch with his bad ankle. This caused sharp pains to shoot through his ankle even more.

I looked over across the field and saw him bent over, wobbling far worse than before, his arms swaying around, and he started hopping on his strong leg with the good ankle. From the looks of it, I seriously thought he broke it; that's how much pain he was in. I grabbed our daughter who was ten years old at the time, and we ran to see what happened. He told me and described how it felt—like needles were shooting all around that bad ankle. He wanted to do nothing but leave at that point. He didn't want to answer any more questions. He was through with the trip to the park and said he was making his way to the car.

Before I could think twice, it just fell out of my mouth. I asked him if he believed that God could heal him. He was kind of tickled that I would ask him such a question. He is a Christian minister whom most would describe as being seasoned when it comes to the scriptures. But nonetheless, I asked him if he believed, and he looked at me in return, wondering if I was serious. It is so funny thinking back on this moment and the look of wonder on his face as to why I would even say that.

He said, "Of course I believe God can heal me."

I said, "Great, because I am going to pray now for this pain to leave."

He couldn't believe it. I couldn't believe I was doing it either. I didn't think much; I just stepped out in faith. I knelt to the ground in the middle of the park, forgetting all the people who were all around us. I laid my hand on his ankle. I asked God to heal and break the pain off His servant, I rebuked the pain, and released the healing power of Jesus over the joints, ligaments, and muscles. I kept thinking how he travels for ministry and needed to be able to walk freely to do what God had assigned Him to do.

I stood up and asked him how he was feeling. He said, "It still hurts" in a frustrating voice. "Okay, thanks, let's go," and he tried to wobble past me.

I didn't give up though. I told him to twirl his ankle around three times. He twirled it around, and by the third twirl, he noticed a heat around his ankle and the pain immediately dissipated. He was in complete shock. His eyes opened wide, he looked at me and said loudly, "What did you do?"

I looked at him with a smile and said, "You know that was not me. It's Jesus." Then I heard in my heart, and I repeated to my husband,

"God has just shown you that you walked with that pain for months and didn't have to."

We rejoiced in the park. My husband even took a joy run in celebration of what God did. Then we sat at a nearby bench and just paused in amazement as we watched the kids play. God can be everything we need if we allow Him. If we choose to get out of our own limited way of thinking, we can experience overall bliss through Jesus. Yielding completely to the One who favors us.

Psalms 3:8 says, "*Salvation belongs to the Lord. Your blessing is upon Your people. Selah.*"

My family: Dameon Jr. (son), Me, Elisha (son), Dameon Sr., and Salah (daughter) Michigan.

TUESDAY, JANUARY 28, 2020

I mentioned in this chapter what happened to me and my experience with food poisoning years ago. I'm reminded of what recently happened at a church. My husband was in a department meeting on a Tuesday night, January 28, 2020. There were rumors about COVID-19 in other countries, but it had not yet hit our area. The meeting ran over a bit. I sat in the fellowship hall waiting for the meeting to end so we could head home. It was almost 10:00 p.m. One of the mothers of the church was in the kitchen area, so I spoke to her and asked her how she was doing.

She said, "Not so well," and that she had food poisoning. She had not been able to eat for days.

I thought of my experience with food poisoning those years ago. She was going into details of how horrible she's been feeling and how it has been very difficult to keep her strength up without being able to eat food. My mind started to race with thoughts of asking to pray for her. This always happens to me—every time I'm about to ask to pray for someone, I immediately get nervous, thinking, "What if they say no?" How I don't want to make anyone feel uncomfortable and how awkward that'll be. But that's never enough to keep me from asking. I remember my grandfather's story in these moments: "What if Jesus wants to heal her? What if just standing in faith with her turn's things around?" So, I gave it a go.

I told her what happened to me when I had food poisoning and how God healed me. I figured that would be a good introduction to asking her if I could pray for her, and much to my relief, she agreed that it was a good idea. I asked her if I could lay my hand on her stomach, and then we stood in agreement for that sickness to leave in Jesus' name. I was at a loss for words and can't remember exactly what I said, but I do remember commanding the poison to leave her body in Jesus' name.

Nothing happened. She still felt poorly, and we were both tired as we were waiting for that meeting to end. She thanked me for offering to pray, then we all went home. The next day, she sent me a message saying that to her surprise, she was finally able to eat something, and it stayed down! Thanks to God. The effects of the food poisoning were leaving, she said she was at 90 percent and was believing God that she would soon be completely healed.

Not all miracles are instant. Some take time. I experienced food poisoning leaving immediately, but the mother from the church went home and noticed the next day she was able to keep down food. She went through a progressive healing. She responded in faith, believing that she was healed even before she saw it. That's the kind of faith we must have.

Like the ten men with leprosy in Luke 17:11-17. Jesus sent the men with leprosy to the priest before they were healed. They had so much faith and trust to just go and follow Jesus's instructions without seeing the evidence of their problems resolved. As they went, Jesus healed them on the way. There was something they had to do first, an act of faith, then the miracle happened. Miracles are activated when someone believes. Prayer is so powerful; believing in God to do it for us is key and believing is the action. This is not always easy to do, but when it is not up to us (which is pretty much always), there is no other choice but to yield to however God wants to walk us through to wholeness.

God deals with each of us according to where we are in faith, and it could just be that He knows the process that's best for us. Healing is not always just physical either. Some healings need to take place in our thinking first. I envision a ripe piece of fruit. It is grown and ready to harvest. Like the outsides of an orange, for example, it must be peeled before enjoying. We all know there is sweetness on the inside, but it is a process to reach that sweet spot. It is all worth it when it is all said and done. It is worth it when we do the work to reach what's on the inside of us. It is so worth it to continue to contend for what we are seeking God to do in us spiritually, physically, and emotionally. This is what I learned: never give up. All things are working together for good to them that love God, to them who are the called according to his purpose (Romans 8:28).

PRAYER AND ACTIVATION:

Everyone's story is different; we are all on unique paths. It is for certain that we all are here for a reason, with a calling and a purpose. God knows what that purpose is and aligns us. If you are on a journey to know God more and want to align to have an encounter with Him, let's pray for that to happen now. Let's talk to the Father together:

Dear Heavenly Father,

Thank You for loving all of us so much that You gave us Jesus (John 3:16). Forgive me of all sins that Satan has tried to use to separate me from You (Colossians 1:21). I believe that Jesus died, rose, and lives forever. I receive the gift of the cross and life everlasting (Ephesians 2:8-9). Come now, Holy Spirit, and fill me completely. Align my life.
I want a supernatural adventure with You. You are the God of miracles; I yield so that You can do a complete work in me right now. I take on my inheritance as a child of the King, an Heir with You, and a joint heir with Christ (Romans 8:17). I am confident that no weapon formed against me shall prosper from this day on (Isaiah 54:17). I stand in faith and break every curse that was spoken against me. I receive only Your promises for my life (Jeremiah 29:11). I set my hands to do Your will in faith. I surrender my desires, my emotions, my future, my all to You.
You are the love that my soul has been longing for. I found You, or rather realized that You've always been there, and I will not let go. May my life never be the same from this moment on.
In Jesus' name. Amen.

Chapter Two

FEBRUARY MIRACLES

"Not by might nor by power, but by My Spirit,' Says the Lord of hosts."
Zechariah 4:6

God delights to use normal people like you and me to reach and encourage our world. Throughout history, we hear countless moments of believers experiencing the move of the Holy Spirit. The Bible teaches us so much. Those written accounts are still happening today. It never stopped. Everyone who has chosen to seek after God with all their heart and with pure motives, have in some way experienced a miracle or know someone who was directly impacted by one. Miracles can come in unexpected moments and circumstances. We should always expect a supernatural move of God. When prayer becomes a habit, miracles can become our lifestyle.

SUNDAY BAPTISM
SUNDAY, FEBRUARY 2, 2020

This day was so special. My children, Dameon Jr, Salah, and Elisha, were baptized all on the same day. This had been something on our minds to do for years—the customary baptism, which is separate from the baby christening. This time, they are of age and know what baptism symbolizes. Baptism represents the death, burial, and resurrection of Jesus. So, as they were lowered into the water, they knew it meant being crucified and buried with Him. And when pulled up from the water, they rose up in new life.

Galatians 2:20 says, "*I have been crucified with Christ; it is no longer I who live, but Christ lives in me; and the life which I now live in the flesh I live by faith in the Son of God, who loved me and gave Himself for me.*" Notice the location of this verse (2:20 lines up with the date, 2/20, for this day of baptism. This day (February 2, 2020) so happens to be the first global palindrome day in 909 years. Palindrome means it can be written the same backward and forwards. It was just unique and stood out to me. I was so excited! God speaks to us all in different ways. When He shows me numbers, dates, or repeated patterns, it becomes a confirmation for me. I take it as a kiss from God, and I blow kisses right back, love on Him and take time to thank Him for grabbing my attention. I love math, God sometimes uses things that relate to us to speak to us. Isn't that so awesome.

I notice patterns—like for my kid's birthdays. They were all given different due dates, but as I laid in labor with our youngest son in the hospital, I knew when he would be born, and I shared this with my husband. The doctors said one thing, but I knew because of what Holy Spirit confirmed in my heart.

Salah was born February 3, 2005 (month 2 + day 3 = '05),
Dameon Jr. was born September 1, 2010 (month 9 + day 1 = '10),
and Elisha was born March 9, 2012 (month 3 + day 9 = '12).

Their 2-digit birth month added to the 2-digit day, equals the 2-digit year they were born. I love God's math.

It was always on my heart to be in the will of God, and when I desired children, my husband and I wanted to make sure it was the right time. As I prayed for our children's purpose and callings, God showed me their birth dates. I feel it was God sending confirmation to wake up my thinking. My children being here had everything to do with Him; that's why they arrived when they did. I don't know all of what they will do and be. But I gave them to God while they were still in the womb, and they belong to Him. Let's pay attention to the subtle ways God speaks to us. Even in the little things, it all matters.

When I prayed about the day of their baptism, I was led to Habakkuk 2:2, "*Then the LORD said to me, 'Write my answer plainly on tablets, so that a runner can carry the correct message to others.'*" I understood it as: our children are going to run for the Kingdom of God, not running away from their calling, and going after righteousness and holiness, without which no man can see the Lord (Hebrews 12:14). They will run successfully and be equipped as we train them to go into all the world and share about our Jesus (Mark 16:15). My prayer is that we as parents will train our children up in the Lord, teach them by being godly examples in front of them, and trust God to fulfill His purpose as we pray over them. Our children are predestined to do the works of the Lord. God knew them even before they were formed in the womb.

TUESDAY, FEBRUARY 18, 2020

The news was flooding with updates on the COVID-19 virus that was spreading in other parts of the world. February is my birthday month, so I was planning to go on a dream cruise with one of my childhood best friends. We share the same birth month and thought it would be cool to celebrate our fortieths visiting tropical islands. Although there were barely any reports in the U.S. at that time, considering the rumors of the virus spreading and the repeating of earthquakes where the cruise ship was supposed to dock, my husband and I agreed to cancel my ticket and offer it to someone else.

This cruise was scheduled to travel to different countries. There was news of another cruise ship that was stuck out in the middle of the ocean because of a breakout of COVID cases. This was so scary and because these were uncertain times, I believe we made the wise decision. I was really looking forward to going and really felt bad that I was no longer considering this trip, but I had to make the best decision for me and my family. The last thing I needed was to be stuck out in the ocean somewhere because of COVID and quarantining.

I had been planning that trip for over six months. Everyone told me to try and get the money I spent back, but that didn't work either. This was completely out of my control. I wanted to pout so badly, but I chose to just stop focusing on that loss. I kept reminding myself in the back of my mind that all things work together for the good. Then amazing things started to happen.

My boss called me into his office and gave me a promotion, which I was totally not expecting. So, although my trip was canceled, I felt like God was giving me a hug for making the right decision. Then I had an interesting dream that same week on a Tuesday.

In the dream I was at a pajama party, many women were there, like in a hall of some sorts. I recognized an old classmate from my grade school years. Her name starts with a "Q" and is pronounced Kee-ana. I have not seen her in over twenty years, and when we were in school, I barely knew her. But there she was in my dream; she stood right in front of me, asking if I could pray for her left shoulder, that she was in a lot of pain and tired of taking medication for it. I prayed for her, and the pain immediately went away. We celebrated and rejoiced in Jesus.

I woke up out of my sleep still rejoicing. There was a song in my heart, "Give your heart to Jesus, / give your heart to Jesus, / give your heart to Jesus, / He will make you whole."

I started to pray for healing for shoulder pains because of what I saw in my dream. I tried to search and reach out to that classmate I saw in my dream, thinking I'd check to see if she needed prayers for her arm. I wanted to confirm what I saw in my dream was true. But nothing became of that search. I knew it was not a coincidence for me to have a dream of a person I have not seen or spoken to in decades. I wrote down the dream in hopes of more clarity in the future and continued in prayer.

FRIDAY, FEBRUARY 21, 2020

That Friday, a few days after the dream of praying for my schoolmate's arm, was my original date to go to the cruise I canceled. My husband was invited to speak for an event that night at our church. Since I was no longer traveling, I went along with him. While we were driving, my husband told me that it was a women's lock-in event. That meant ladies were gathering at the church and planning to stay there all night. I thought to myself, "Well, that sounds like a pajama party! A sleepover like in my dream. What if someone's there who would need to be healed in their shoulder?" I had no idea, but what was to come blew my mind.

My husband preached, and it was so amazing. Many said their hearts were pricked and felt healing as he taught on the power of forgiveness and letting go of issues from our childhood. After his message, we all prayed together in the fellowship hall. Then the floor was yielded for all the other activities lined up for that night. But one of the mothers of the church announced that if anyone wanted to continue in prayer, to head over to the sanctuary. It was around fifteen of us who wanted to pray more. We took turns praying for all that God placed on our hearts. I remembered the dream and told my husband that maybe I should ask if someone needs healing in their shoulder. This is kind of scary to do. What if I ask and there is no response? Well, I'm willing to take a risk. My husband encouraged me to go ahead and ask, so I mustered up some courage, took the mic from him, asked if anyone had shoulder pains, and if they would like prayer. There was an odd silence for a few seconds. I thought maybe no one would say a word. Then I heard a voice from the back of the church.

A lady I never met raised her hand and said she needed prayer for her shoulder. She was praying in the back of the church and walked up to the front where we were. I was relieved, of course. She and I started conversing and as I started to share my dream with her, I noticed her name badge. We all were wearing them that night. I had not seen her name until that moment. I asked her to pronounce her name. I thought surely my eyes could be playing tricks on me. It was the same sound as the person in my dream. But her name started with a "K," and was Keeana. I stood there with my jaw dropped and looked to my husband and told him it was the same name as in my dream. This has never happened to me before! I had to collect myself and go ahead and tell her what I saw and how I'd been praying for someone with her name and with her ailment. She needed prayer for her left shoulder, just like in the dream. It dawned on me that God had given me a word of knowledge for someone I had never met. Someone I would meet days later. God used something that I was familiar with so that I would intercede for someone I would meet in the future. The Holy Spirit is truly amazing.

Word of knowledge by the Holy Spirit is when there is a specific piece of information or knowledge that God reveals to us. This information is something for the present time or past that we did not know on our own, but God reveals it to us. In a nutshell, this is information that can be for someone regarding healing, a word to encourage them, or even a word for guidance. Again, this is revealed to us by God and was not previous knowledge or information we came up with by ourselves. First Corinthians 12:7-8 reads, "*A spiritual gift is given to each of us so we can help each other. To one person the Spirit gives the ability to give wise advice; to another the same Spirit gives a message of special knowledge.*" God revealed several things to me in that dream: a lady's pajama party (or lock-in), a name, and that a left shoulder would be healed.

After explaining everything to Keeana, she started to cry and shared how she'd been praying for so long for so many things, how she'd laid things before God and had been waiting on Him. I laid my hand on her shoulder and thanked God for revealing what would happen and for having me pray for her even before knowing who she was. I thanked God for being so loving. He knew her and wanted her to be healed.

I commanded the pain to leave in the name of Jesus. I spoke to her arm, the joints, the tissues, the muscles, and told the spirit of pain to leave in the name of Jesus. Several of us had tears in our eyes by then. After praying, I asked her to test it out, and she started to swing her arm around like a windmill and declared there was no pain. All of us who were in the sanctuary witnessed this miracle. I told them all that I was not supposed to be there that evening. That I had planned a cruise trip that was divinely canceled. God made sure of it the week before because He wanted me to deliver this message and prayer to Keeana personally. My dream cruise was replaced with a dream from God that led me to a lady who had been suffering for twenty years with this shoulder pain.

It is not a coincidence that I had not seen the person in my dreams in over twenty years, and Keeana had been suffering with her pain for about twenty years. Wow! I don't know about anyone else, but I prefer the will and dreams of God to be fulfilled more than anything else in the world. That experience exceeded any birthday wish I could have ever thought of. And I would have missed it had I gone with my plans and not the leading of the Holy Spirit, being in the right place at the right time.

Lord, please lead us so we can always be in the right place at the right time. Partnering with the Holy Spirit makes for an exciting life. Here is a testimony and picture Keeana gave me permission to share.

Testimony

I had been having a very difficult time, where it felt like everyone I loved was under attack. I had been praying and begging God to intervene and take all the pain away, but I felt like He wasn't listening. I mean, I knew God was always there, but it felt as if He wasn't hearing me. Fast forward to February, and I was invited to the Mother's Lock-In at my church. I

went into the sanctuary to pray. While I was praying, Elisha asked if anyone had any shoulder pain. Now I've seen both her and her husband ministering at church, but we had never spoken before. Her question stunned me because I've had this pain in my left shoulder for about twenty years. It started in college out of nowhere. It is nothing I've even ever complained to my doctor about. I've just always lived with it. I started not to say anything but decided to speak up. Elisha asked for my name, and when I told her, she said that the Lord brought my name up to her in a dream and that she had been praying for me. She laid hands on my shoulder, prayed, and I have been pain-free since! But even more than that, her obedience to the Holy Spirit to even ask if anyone had shoulder pain—and telling me that God placed me on her heart, let me know that God HAD been listening! He was paying such close attention to me that He decided to heal me from something I never even asked for! So of course, He was going to meet my needs concerning what I've been asking for!
Keeana (holding up healed shoulder). Michigan.

HEALED FROM SPEECH DELAY

More healings took place at the Women's Lock-In at the church on that Friday night. So many wonderful things happened as we all were walking about praying for each other. One of the ladies named Yasmin witnessed how God was moving and asked me to pray for her son (Houston) who she said was behind in speech. He was three years old at the time. She was in tears as she explained what the doctors had said to her about his development. I'm a mother, so I can understand the concern she was feeling.

I hugged her and I told her we certainly could pray. Let's give it to God! He can do all things. Little Houston was just playing and roaming about as little ones do. We finally caught up with him and his mother sat him on the altar. We sat down close together with him, and I laid my hands on his head and touched his little mouth and commanded his tongue to be loosened, for him to talk clearly, for his speech to catch up and flourish. I've also never done this before; that night was full of a lot of firsts for me. I canceled the spirit that came to cause delay, distraction, and progression in Jesus' name. He wanted to play more, so we kept it short and let him go and continue to play amongst us. We went on, but I glimpsed over at little Houston as we were praying, and he was so happy and full of smiles.

I didn't find out that night, but according to Houston's mom, that night there was a noticeable change in his speech. Some ladies were talking about this wonderful move of God on social media, and they tagged me in a conversation that blew my mind. Her son was talking clearly for the first time. She was blown away and so was I. Can you imagine your son not being able to talk and suddenly he starts talking clearly? Wow, glory to Jesus!

I saw her rejoicing and dancing as we continued with prayers that night. But I would soon find out that God took away her sorrow and worry. As mothers, we love our babies. It is hard to watch them suffer from anything. The love of a true mother is like none other. The best thing we can do is give our little innocent babies to God just like Yasmin did that night, laying him on the altar. The adversary goes after our seed, tries to apply spiritual limitations on them early. It is because he knows their future is promising, through the power of God in their lives. We as parents must keep our children before the Father. Houston was healed because his mother had been praying for him and laid her concerns at His feet. The enemy thought he could steal from this family, but John 10:10 says, "*A thief has only one thing in mind—he wants to steal, slaughter, and destroy. But I have come to give you everything in abundance, more than you expect—life in its fullness until you overflow*!" This is just the beginning for Houston and his mom, a beautiful healing through Jesus, overflowing in all things. I asked Yasmin to explain what happened that night. Here is a testimony and picture of her son she gave permission to share. Glory to Jesus forever.

Testimony

Words can't express how grateful I am to God. My son was three years old and couldn't formulate sentences like most kids his age. I had been praying, but it seemed like nothing had changed. Even though I was praying, I didn't believe until Elisha held us close in her arms in prayer. The energy that was exchanged was a moment of transparency and love. We laid my child on the altar, and

she prayed over my son. God did the miraculous right in that moment; my son's words became clear. Hallelujah! Thank you, Jesus!
Houston. Michigan

ALL-CONSUMING FIRE

After a while, a few of us lined up at the front of the church to pray for anyone who wanted to come forward. An elderly lady walked toward me without saying anything about what she wanted to pray for. I wish I would have caught her name. With everything that was happening that night, after a while, we got lost in His amazing presence. As this dear lady stood in front of me, I grabbed her hands and started to pray for the Holy Spirit to move on her behalf. He knows her situation and has the power to apply the solution.

Not long in the prayer, I was led to wrap my arms around her. I hugged her and continued in prayer. I listened and opened my heart to pray what the Holy Spirit wanted for her. Pain came to my mind, so I began to speak to a spirit of pain. I commanded it to leave her body. From the crown of her head to the soles of her feet. I told it to go and report to the feet of Jesus. For the Holy Spirit to come and fill her up.

The Holy Spirit leads us in how to pray when we listen to Him. He connects with our spirits, heals our emotions, but also our physical bodies. Our heavenly Father desires to embrace us in His arms. Like how I wrapped my arms around this lady. I knew in that moment that God loved her so much, and I wanted her to know it. God wanted her to know it. As I commanded the pain to leave, she began to shake all over in my arms. It was like a wave of His power swept through her entire body. She seemed so reserved earlier but could no longer be still with His love flowing from the inside out. God's heart for her was being revealed.

James 4:8 says, "*Draw near to God and He will draw near to you.*" We can come to God at any moment, right now where we are, church, home, school—it doesn't matter. He wants us to come to Him. The end part of that scripture says, "*Cleanse your hands, you sinners; and purify your hearts, you double-minded.*" For all the limitations to be broken off, for us to receive in full what God has for us, we must repent and stay away from what is considered unclean. The Holy Spirit wants to flow freely through us but cannot do so in a willfully unclean temple.

After the prayer, the elderly lady was full of smiles and walked away rejoicing. We asked if there were any testimonies or experiences anyone wanted to share. She raised her hand and informed us that she had pain all over her body when she came. As I was praying for her and was led to speak directly for pain to leave, she felt the power of God flow through and remove it all. She had been to the doctors, and several tests were run to try to figure out why she was in pain all over. She was given medicines to make her comfortable, but nothing helped.

This is an interesting thing. I've noticed that when doctors cannot find a diagnosis, often the issue is caused by an evil spirit. As we stood in prayer of agreement, she believed and had faith and experienced the hand of God. John 14:13 says, "*You can ask for anything in my name, and I will do it, so that the Son can bring glory to the Father.*"

It is important to understand that although this lady went to the doctors, she still sought help from God. It is not always the case that doctors can't find a diagnosis, but I've learned from praying for several people that it could be an indication of a spiritual attack. Doctors are a blessing to our world and many of them are used by God and see miracles themselves. They are mentioned throughout the Bible. The only mistake we can make as believers is to trust more in medicine than in God. Second Chronicles 16:12 shares a story of King Asa, who was afflicted with a disease in his feet. He did not seek the Lord for help; he only went to doctors who practiced medicine. And in those days, they mixed medicine with superstitions and folk remedies. It is not a good thing to open the door to occult resources or pseudo-medical treatments. We must be careful not to go that route.

Our ultimate focus is to have faith in God. Do not avoid doctors but pray in addition to going. Doctors do their research and can give a diagnosis. But we must remember that a diagnosis is not the final say. God is the chief physician. We can take those same diagnoses and do what James 5:14-15 says, "*Are any of you sick? You should call for the elders of the church to come and pray over you, anointing you with oil in the name of the Lord. Such a prayer offered in faith will heal the sick, and the Lord will make you well. And if you have committed any sins, you will be forgiven.*"

Do not let a sickness or diagnosis keep you from God. Stand on His Word. Like this lady did, she in turn experienced the all-consuming fire of God. Hallelujah!

A DREAM OF PREGNANCY

I am just in utter amazement. The Women's Lock-In event turned into opportunities for healings and miracles to happen. It all started from a dream earlier that week. A dream that gave me a word of knowledge and revealed what would happen later that week. God's plans are so awesome, and He speaks in dreams. I am reminded of an experience I had on July 14, 2016.

One of my friends and sister in Christ was pregnant in my dream. I know it could sound funny, but sometimes God shows me pictures of people and just by seeing them, I know all about that moment. Her and her husband had a little girl and were not planning for more children at that time of the dream. But I saw it clear as day, and I knew that she was carrying a boy. When I wake from dreams like these, I always pray and ask God if there are any other meanings. I took note of the dream as is my custom, writing it in my dreams journal (we should have a prophecy, dreams, and healing journal to keep track of things), and I felt led to send her a text message about it that day. I also told her that this baby boy will be a blessing to the Kingdom, and to be encouraged because God is in all the plans. She gladly received the message, and we went on with our everyday life. It was exactly one year later to the day that she had a doctor's appointment and they confirmed that she was with child.

She shared the good news with my husband and I. The Holy Spirit reminded me of the message I sent her, so I went to see if I still had the text message in my phone. I had only spoken to her a few times through text over the year, so the message was pretty easy to find. And there it was, time stamped and confirmed. The date leaped out to me—I gasped and immediately told her. We knew this could not be a coincidence. I am happy I was able to share with her the dream. I held on to the fact that she would be having a very special and brilliant little boy. Her friends planned a baby reveal party. I was so excited to attend but felt I had the inside scoop! The results confirmed that she was indeed having a boy. He is here now and thriving glory to God. I am so happy I journaled this experience. It is so special how God speaks to us. It is so important to listen and take notes as God can show us things to encourage others, giving clarity of what's happening now or of future events. Remember we are here for reasons bigger than ourselves.

SUNDAY, FEBRUARY 23, 2020

We were still on a spiritual high from all the miracles that were happening that week. I went to church thinking "Wow, anything can happen today." I wanted to scream from a mountaintop all the stuff that happened. I ended up crying a lot during worship, just thinking about how much God loves us. I am overwhelmed at His sovereignty. After church on Sunday, one of the mothers that attended the lock-in called me over to talk with a lady named Tammy who was a singer on the music team. Tammy was having back problems and pains all during the time we were at the church. We shared how, at the lock-in, God moved in power, and we believed that God could do it again.

While Tammy was explaining her pain, I thought to myself how Jesus was there with us, and I prayed within myself to be bold and represent what Jesus would do in that moment. I asked Tammy if she could rate her pain from 1-10, ten being the worst pain. Tammy said the pain was a very high level, but when she removed her shoes and sat down to try to get some relief, the pain dropped to around a five. I asked if I could pray for her, to believe with her for the pain to leave. She agreed, and then I asked her to point to the area where the pain was. The church mother and I joined together and prayed for Tammy's back pain to leave. We commanded the muscles, the tissues, the bones, the joints, the spine, and the nerves to all line up and be healed in the name of Jesus. We probably prayed for one or two minutes. People were gathering up their things and heading out of the church. After the prayer, I asked her if she could find any pain, to test it out. She tested it out and said there was no pain and that she felt so much better. I asked her to twist and to bend to make sure. Glory to Jesus! Here are her words and a picture she gave permission to share.

Testimony

I thank God! I have heard Elisha speak and sing, but personally, I've witnessed her healing gift. I sought her out one Sunday after service and asked her to pray for me. She unreservedly lay hands on me and prayed for the situation. Immediately I felt a calmness and difference. I felt better and light. She is a quiet storm, and I thank God for

her.

Tammy. Michigan.

MONDAY, FEBRUARY 24, 2020

The following Monday was my birthday. I had a few non-working days because I was planning to be gone for the entire week. But God changed my plans, and I could not be more excited and happier about it. I was going to go back to work to do some engineering projects later that week, but I received an interesting call from my modeling agency where I do commercial, runway, print, and billboard advertisements. I did not know that God had more amazing supernatural things in store. The agent asked if I was free that week to travel up north. I informed them of how my plans changed; I was supposed to be out of town, but now my week was open. They told me that a hotel and casino wanted to book me for advertising. I would have to spend a day traveling to get there to get checked in and settled. They wanted to book me for four days—two days to model so they could gather footage for the commercial, and the other two days for traveling. Normally I would audition for opportunities like these, and honestly, would not consider a casino. But the Holy Spirit led me to see that this was no coincidence. I prayed and took a closer look at the details. I was supposed to be gone the entire week, but those plans were canceled. This hotel wanted to hire me solely from seeing my image on the agency portal, and the money they offered me was four times over the amount I paid for the cruise trip that I lost. I did not see this coming! I thought I was going to miss out when I canceled that trip. Instead, I have seen several miracles breaking out—what is God up to?

I thought to myself, "Who is at this hotel that God wants me to meet? Will miracles happen?" Like when I went to the Women's Lock-In. This offer just fell into my lap and the pay was quite generous. He put on my heart that everywhere we go as believers should be viewed as a mission for Him. That He is not limited to the four walls of the church; He wants to reach people in all areas of life. I accepted the offering and prepared my mind that this was a modeling missions' trip. I am going to model after Christ. To be ready for Kingdom encounters and to shine the light of Jesus.

Be it in season or out of season, in a church, or out of the church or even in a casino. I want to represent Him well. Our focus as we worship the Father should not be about worshiping in the right place, but rather having the right heart according to John 4:24, "For God is a Spirit, so those who worship him must worship in spirit and in truth." When we yield to God, we set ourselves up to experience His glory in any place. God is everywhere and wants to reach the world. He just needs a willing vessel to step out in faith; then He does all the rest of the work.

Because of the attitude that I had towards the sudden change of plans this week, I felt as though the Father rewarded me greatly. It was, after all, still a nice, paid-in-full, getaway trip with hundreds of dollars per-diem, which was in addition to the overall rate for the four days—delicious foods cooked by great chefs and networking with production companies and other actors and models. God blessed me with more than I could have ever expected during the week of my birthday!

When I checked into my room the first day, I started to pray for God to lead me to someone who would need prayer. I thought of Jesus. If He were there, would He only hang around the churches? No. He would be in the casinos, the bars, the jailhouses—everywhere—to reach all people. In Luke 5:27-32, Jesus ate and spent time with people who needed to know Him. Not to say that everyone does not know Him in these places. The Pharisees criticized Him for this, but He was doing something right. I thought about that as I stood in the lobby and took walks around the casino. I waited for the Holy Spirit to highlight someone to me. This is the everyday expectation I feel God wants me to have. We are equipped to reach our world for Jesus. And often we miss opportunities because of feeling inadequate or unqualified or worried of what someone would think. Also, we miss out when our plans get in the way of His plans.

I reminded myself of 2 Peter 1:3, which says, "*Everything we could ever need for life and godliness has already been deposited in us by his divine power. For all this was lavished upon us through the rich experience of knowing him who has called us by name and invited us to come to him through a glorious manifestation of his goodness.*"

He resides in us, and that goodness can be released on those around us to win the lost for Christ. I waited around and was a little nervous to approach people because I know not everyone is coming to the casino for prayer; they might think I am nuts. The first person I prayed for was a lady who walked in with a cast on her leg. I approached her and told her I was a Christian minister, and I asked her about her leg. She told me she got into a ski accident and that she was hoping it would mend together okay and heal quickly. I asked her if I could pray for those things she mentioned. She was shocked but smiled and was kind enough to let me pray for her. I asked her if I could place my hand on the cast, and she gave me permission to do that. So, I prayed in the lobby of the casino, in front of bystanders, and released the power of Jesus to remove the pain and that her leg would heal fast in Jesus's name.

I looked at her, she smiled and said, "Thank you," and then hurried to catch up with her friends. I did not get a chance to ask her how she felt (she ran off so fast), but when she walked in the lobby, she was favoring that leg, and when she walked away, she wasn't walking so gently. I just know that our encounter was a God one and she and I felt it. It was quite the experience, sitting in the lobby, listening for the Holy Spirit and crossing paths with all these new faces that God loves.

I met a lot of amazing people working on the crew for the commercial as well. This included another lady who was hired to do voiceovers and acting. I did not know she was a popular DJ for a prestigious country station in our city. After working together, we exchanged information, and she saw that I was a spirit lifestyle coach and the testimonies of healings and miracles that I shared on social media. God is always up to more than we can imagine or think. This DJ eventually started having prayers on the country station and invited me to be the person to pray every week.

We must be open to yield to God's plans and not our own. Being in partnership with the Holy Spirit causes us to enjoy God, and for Him to enjoy us. It can be scary sometimes because we do not know what's coming next. But that is the beauty of it! Letting Him do the hard thinking for us and trusting Him along the way. He dwells in us. We carry His glory; we are Kingdom ambassadors. Like 1 Corinthians 3:16 says, "*Don't you realize that together you have become God's inner sanctuary and that the Spirit of God makes his permanent home in you?*" No matter where He calls us, if we are bold enough to follow Him, dropping our plans for Him, mind-blowing things will start to occur. If I did not come, I would not have connected with the country station to share prayers for healings and miracles. I am all too excited to see what else is to come.

Behind-the-scenes footage of me and the crew on set in the casino hotel Saganing, Michigan.

PRAYER AND ACTIVATION:

Plans change and things will not always be what we expect it to be. But when we are in relationship with God, it is okay. What God wants is all that matters. All things will work together for the good of those who love the Lord and who are called according to His purpose. We do not want to miss out by fighting against God's plans or trying to please others. If you want to commit to His ways and allow Him to work miracles in your life, let us ask for that right now. Let us talk to the Father together.

Dear Heavenly Father, thank You for Your goodness and for Your thoughtfulness towards us (Psalms 100:5). I want to commit my dreams, goals, ambitions and all my plans to You.
I am sorry if I've tried to go ahead of You. I am sorry if I've gotten frustrated with You because things didn't go as I planned. Lord, help me to trust how You navigate my life (Proverbs 3:5-6). You are, after all, the Author of it all.
What You want for me is all that matters. I want Your will, not my own (Matthew 7:21). I care about what You care about, not what others think. You make the best choices for me, and I submit to You fully (James 4:7-10).
Thank You for working miracles in my life, for keeping me rooted and grounded in Your Word (Ephesians 3:17-19). I walk in preordained paths, my carnal mind is not in control of me, and my spirit is one with Yours (1 Corinthians 6:17). You lead me in the way everlasting (Psalms 139:23-24).
I reflect Your light, divine health, and prosperity, causing me to live my best life no matter where I am or what I am doing. Everyone I cross paths

with will see the reflection of You like a mirror (2 Corinthians 3:18). Wonders will take place not by my might, not by my power, but by Your Spirit (Zechariah 4:6). Whether it is in dreams while my head is resting on a pillow fast asleep or awake, going about the day.
I am a dispenser of Your glory. In Jesus' name, amen.

Chapter Three

MARCH MIRACLES

"Do not be slothful in zeal, be fervent in spirit, serve the Lord." Romans 12:11

AMAZED BY THE HOLY SPIRIT

From one excitement to the next, for years I had a great passion for the Holy Spirit. I would share stories of how God moved with friends and family. Every opportunity given, I wanted to share a testimony of the beauty of Jesus and how miracles are still happening all around us. My family is the first to experience my excitement. Especially my children. We would read the stories of how Jesus healed so many. I encouraged them to believe that such things are still happening today. It was not long before I was hearing from one of my son's teachers that my son was holding prayer at school with other students. And he was only in third grade! God can place in our hearts early the desire to serve and to lead others to Christ, who is the answer to our dying world.

LOOKING BACK TO SUNDAY, MARCH 19, 2017

Thinking of how important it is to share our experiences and involve our children in our walk with Jesus, I am reminded of this Sunday some years ago.

After church, my husband and I, along with the kids, went to eat at Longhorn Steakhouse. On the drive from the church to the restaurant, my daughter told me that she would love to see a healing or miracle. At this time, she was twelve years old, and would often hear me share the testimonies of how God would move. You can never really gauge when something like this would happen, and so far, it has been in moments when she was not in the same vicinity.

She said, "Mom, I want to see someone get healed. I am never around when you pray for someone for a miracle."

I told her that if it is the desire of her heart, then God will allow her to start to see many miracles. That is how it started for me. I was young like her when I first wanted to see God move supernaturally. We made it to the restaurant and ordered our food, and my daughter and I went to the ladies' room to freshen up. In the bathroom, we started to talk about the dress I ordered off Amazon. It was vintage styled, and my daughter really liked it. She took my picture with her iPhone, and I posed—you know, the typical stuff girls do when they go to the ladies' room! We washed our hands and headed back to the table. We walked out and took our seats, but then suddenly heard a lot of commotion and yelling. A lady fell as she walked out of the ladies' room. She was lying in between tables unresponsive, and her daughter, who seemed to be close to my age, was hysterically screaming. I caught eyes with my husband, and he nodded in approval as though he knew my thoughts already. I was indeed thinking to pray for her.

So, in that very same dress I was just taking pictures in, without even thinking twice, I rushed over to where she was laying and got on my hands and knees beside her. Someone called an ambulance. It was kind of interesting to see the reaction of the people sitting around her. She was laying in between two tables where people were sitting. They just looked down at her when she fell and did not move a muscle. One guy raised his hand to get the server' attention. By that time, I was on the floor with the lady. I honestly did not know what was going on. It is scary when someone falls like that. Was she still breathing? Was she slipping away?

I just called on Jesus for her. I started to pray, and a few minutes later another lady got on her knees beside me, standing in agreement. I then felt someone's hand on my back. A man dressed in a suit walked over and started to stand in agreement with us. I went from being scared for her to feeling the strength of the Lord and believing for her recovery. The lady we were praying for went from laying unresponsive to grabbing her chest, then she whispered that she could not breathe. She continued to hold her hand to her chest, appearing to be in pain. It seemed to get even worse. She started to jerk in a spasm sort of way. All I could think of was a heart attack. I placed my hand on her hand which was laying on her chest and commanded her heart to function properly in the name of Jesus. That her airways would open, that every artery, every valve in the heart, every organ, all muscles, all nerves, all blood flow would be healed and function normally. That all the pain would leave her body in Jesus' name.

Many people who were sitting around us heard us calling on the name of Jesus. The entire restaurant was silent. The name of Jesus filled the airways. We stayed there and prayed without ceasing. The lady stopped having the spasms and started to breathe normally while her eyes were shut. Then the ambulance showed up, we moved out of the way, and the lady was able to stand and get on the stretcher as the EMS team assisted her. I went back to my table. My family was praying along as well. I sat and watched them take her out of the restaurant, thanking God that she was breathing and seemed to be pain-free. My daughter turned to me and said, "Mom I just asked to see a miracle in the car on the way here, and I just did." I had not thought about that.

Wow, I thought. This is just the beginning for my kids. Because they believe and have a desire to see miracles, they will see many in Jesus' name.

The pictures my daughter took of me that day in the lady's bathroom at the restaurant. The vintage dress. –Longhorn Steakhouse. Michigan.

MONDAY, MARCH 2, 2020

I have learned over time how to share Jesus at work without rubbing people the wrong way. I am an engineer and work with lots of other engineers who come from all different places and beliefs in the world. I talk about work, but I am also known to be open in talking about how good God is to me. To me, there are right and wrong ways of spreading the gospel. So, I am still learning to consciously make a point to allow God to have His way so I don't irritate or rub people the wrong way—sometimes I can be a bit zealous. There is nothing more terrible than pushing too hard, having good intentions but running people away.

One time I was walking into the electrical lab at work and an engineer from India walked in. He had a surgical boot on his foot. He started to share about what happened to his foot, so I thought that would be a good moment to offer prayer. I was nervous to ask but I did. He started to laugh hysterically. Then he suddenly stopped laughing and said, "Oh, you are serious? I am sorry for laughing, but no, you can't pray for my foot."

He was nice about it, but I just felt maybe I missed the mark on that one. I later learned he was Hindu and worshiped Buddha. I just said, "Okay, just thought I'd ask."

He said, "Thanks for asking. You have a nice day," and we went on to continue our work.

The good part is I tried and did not keep pressing when he turned down the prayer. I guess these experiences are good to have because not everyone will want to receive prayer. If God wants it to happen, I believe God will prepare our hearts for that exchange. We do not know when those moments will happen, so it is good to stay ready, to be open, bold, and courageous to pray, and share the love of Jesus. Being led is key, but we are always representing Jesus no matter what. He is seen in our smiles, when we help someone, when we encourage someone, and when we are pleasant to work with.

On Monday, March 2nd, I was working in a conference room. An engineer by the name of Hassib stopped by to chat. We had been having discussions about the Bible for months prior. During lunch, we would catch up on what God has been doing in our lives. He is connected with me on social media where I share testimonies, so he would often ask me questions about that. He saw how I spoke highly of Jesus. This day, he asked me why I always mentioned God, Jesus, and the Holy Spirit, but not the saints and Mary. He wanted to know if I honored them like he did. He wanted to know if I prayed to the saints and if I prayed to Mary, all who are now with the Lord. I showed him scriptures on why I prayed in the name of Jesus. I told him that I believed that Jesus is the only door to the Father, as written in John 14:6. I shared with him how I love all the disciples and Mary; I study their lives from the scriptures and learn so much from them. I honor them and every other apostle, prophet, pastor, preacher, and teacher. But I do not pray to them. It is written in John 10:9 where Jesus said, "*I am the door. If anyone enters in by me, he will be saved...*"

The disciples and Mary preached and prayed in Jesus' name, and so do I. Scripture tells us that there is only one way to enter into the spirit realm—that way being Jesus, who connects us to the supernatural holy realm of God. Prayers to other gods or people, those who are trying to enter the supernatural realm by other means, are tapping into the deceptive realm of Satan. Satan does all he can to try to confuse in this way. He tries to do as much damage as he can while people are enslaved in ideologies, traditions, and false religions.

After sharing some scriptures of how I only pray in the name of Jesus, I reiterated to him that this method is the only way that I have seen results, healings, and miracles. Hassib asked me to give him some examples of that. After sharing how I prayed for people in the prior months, he was very encouraged. It is written in John 14:14, "*Ask me anything in my name, and I will do it.*"

I saw a new look in his eyes, an excitement just from these scriptures. We sat at a table in that little conference room, and it seemed to me that suddenly it was a setup by the Holy Spirit to move. I started to look down at my computer and continue in my work, but Hassib said, "Before you continue back to work, can you pray for me like you prayed for those other people?" He had been having shoulder pains and wanted to see if God could heal him. I thought to myself: this could be an opportunity for Jesus to prove the very scriptures that we just shared. I told him of course we can pray, but I made sure to highlight to him that when I pray for him, I am praying in the name of Jesus. He said okay, and that he understood.

I asked him where the pain was located on his shoulder. He placed his hand on it so I could see. I told him that I would place my hand on that spot and all he needed to do was receive the prayer. I told him that it is God that does the work, it is not me, and that I am only standing in faith with him as we trust God for this pain to leave. So, I touched his shoulder and started to pray.

We prayed and invited the Holy Spirit to come, we repented of past sins, and then we told the pain to leave his body in the name of Jesus. It was a very quick prayer. I would say a maximum of two minutes. He started to look at me with this confused look on his face. So, I asked him how he was feeling. He said that he felt an unusual heat coming from my hand and into his arm. His eyes got big, and he continued to look amazed. I told him that he can have more of that, especially if he dedicates himself solely to God and keeps His commandments. I just stood still and did not want to interrupt anything that God was doing. This was a very beautiful moment. His eyes were open to something new: the truth and nearness of God. That he could go to God for himself when he prays in the name of Jesus.

I held back my tears and remained calm. I told him that the same power in the signs and the wonders that the disciples walked in, the saints, the prophets—we can also walk in that if we believe. I asked him about the pain, and he said he felt the pain leaving his arm. I thanked God and continued to invite the Holy Spirit to fill him up, that his life would never be the same from that moment. He was so shocked that he was touched in that way. His arm stayed warm for some time after we prayed. He got up and was getting ready to go back to work. He turned and said to me, "I'm going to let you know all that happens for me because of Jesus," with the biggest smile on his face. He went his way, and I sat there in a daze.

How can I get back to my engineering work after something like that happens?

Eventually I did, but not before joyfully crying, so blessed and honored to have been there with my coworker as he experienced the hand of God healing his body. Every time I see him at work, I see a changed person. God did more than heal his arm. He removed doubts and opened Hassib's eyes to some Kingdom realities. He started to share his experience and the scriptures we discussed with his family and friends. He told them of the authority we have through Jesus. Some got angry with him, especially the elderly family members. But he is chosen to believe and continue to share in spite of their disapproval, like the disciples. Here is the testimony and picture he gave permission to share.

Testimony

One day we were praying in a conference room where we work. After prayer, I asked Elisha to pray specifically for my shoulder which was hurting me. At that time, I felt the power of God breaking the pain. It was an abnormal heat, so I felt that something had entered my body. It was a delightful feeling of joy, and compassion. I do not know how to describe this feeling, and then I felt that the pain eased and on the next

day I felt better and was happy that the Holy Spirit was the one who changed everything in me.
Hassib and his wife, Loriane. Michigan.

FRIDAY, MARCH 6, 2020

Just when I thought all the birthday celebrating was good and over with—seriously, it is March now—my husband had planned one more big surprise. I woke up Friday, March 6, out of a dream. I dreamt I prayed for someone's lower back, and they were healed instantly. If I find myself dreaming this way, I am learning to get up and just pray for that healing to take place. I could be interceding for someone I have not met yet or may never meet. I might have an encounter with someone throughout the day who is dealing with back pains.

I went on to work and by the time I was leaving, I remembered the dream. I was not led to pray for anyone at work, and no one complained of back pains. I then headed to my kids' school for scheduled parent-teacher conferences. I thought to myself: maybe one of the teachers will need prayer for their back. But it never came up.

When I arrived home, my husband said to change from my work clothes and to dress comfortably. He also told me to pack an overnight bag. He had a nice surprise for me. I was wondering what was going on, where was he taking me, and why would I need an overnight bag? We pulled up to this building. He walked me to the door without saying a word. He opened the door, and I heard voices shout out, "SURPRISE!" Then they started to sing happy birthday.

I could not believe it. My husband rented a loft and invited some of my closest family and friends for a lady's sleepover. Anyone who knows me knows I love butterflies. Everyone was wearing butterfly shirts. I could not believe my husband pulled this off without me finding out! I am so thankful for just a wonderful and thoughtful husband.

My face was probably turning red, and my eyes filled with tears as I made my way around the room to speak to everyone. I took a moment, looked around the room, and saw the faces of all these beautiful women. Not just beautiful on the outside, but I was surrounded by friends who I knew were selfless, Christ – focused, and just as beautiful on the inside.

God's tangible presence as well as inner beauty literally infused the room. The atmosphere was too sweet for words. We hugged, laughed, and just shared in a wonderful time with one another. It was about an hour into the night, we were just starting to have cake, and the Holy Spirit reminded me of the dream of praying for someone's lower back last night. I thought to myself—wow, maybe it was about someone here at the loft.

The music was blaring, and the ladies were conversing amongst each other. I leaned over and whispered to one of my sisters to tell her, "I think I must pray for someone here." She giggled, wondering if I was serious. I told her I couldn't let the night end without at least asking. This would not be that hard, I thought. This room is filled with people I know and love, and I know they love me. So, we turned down the music, and I asked if someone in the room had lower back pains. Two ladies raised their hands. I knew then that something miraculous was going to happen.

40th Birthday Party at the Loft.
L-R: (Grandma) Dorothy, (sister) Micah, Me, (sister) LaKeeta, (Mom) Deborah,(sister-in-law) Jasmine.
Michigan.

I started to share with them about my dream and how I believed once we prayed, the pain would leave. They were all for it, glad to pray. All of us joined in together. I prayed for lower back pains, but several other prayer requests started to come up. I ended up standing in agreement for healing with six ladies. There were reports of migraine headaches leaving. I prayed for knee pains and shoulder pains to leave as well. This wasn't planned, but the birthday party also turned into a miracle hub party! That's so like our Jesus.

One of my cousins was laying down because she had a migraine. After I prayed for others, one of my other cousins told me of the cousin with the migraines. I laid next to her and brushed my finger across her head to move her hair from over her eyes. She opened her eyes and smiled. I told her that I heard she had a migraine headache, and I was wondering if I could pray for it. She set her head up and looked from side to side. She said, "I don't feel the migraine anymore." It was just there and suddenly gone, so she got up and was able to enjoy the rest of the party.

Crazy awesome things like this were happening. I honestly didn't know what in the world was going to happen next. This was a supernatural move of God. I was super excited to experience this with all the ladies I love. One of the ladies named Renata, who had lower back pain I dreamt of, said she had always had the issue, but she learned to live with it. I asked her to sit in a chair, and my mother and I (pictured in the photo) compared the lengths of her legs by lining up her shoes. We noticed that one was a little over an inch longer than the other. I had seen a pastor do that before. Lower back pain that has always been there can be an indication that one leg has always been longer than the other. So, we prayed in the name of Jesus for her legs to be the same length. I know that could be a stretch, but just what if? I prayed that the tissues, muscles, and nerves in her back, all of it, would line up and the pain would leave and report to the feet of Jesus. We also prayed for her shoulder, which had been hurting for a week. God touched her that night. I felt that my dream was for her for sure.

We measured how her shoes lined up as she stretched her legs out and they were the same length, unlike before we prayed. Although I wanted this to happen for her, I was blown away that it did. I felt a rush and a high of joy in the Holy Spirit all night. Hallelujah! God delightfully surprised us. I kept a "Yay to Jesus!" in my heart. Here is a testimony and a picture of Renata that she's given permission to share.

Testimony

I want to share how the Lord healed my body during Elisha's surprise birthday party. Elisha stopped the music and asked if anyone needed prayer for back pain specifically. I raised my hand. She asked me a few questions, then had me sit in a chair. We discovered that my left leg was shorter than the other by 1.5 inches. So, Elisha prayed, and it seemed to level out. She had me test out my pain level. I stood and moved around to try to find the pain, but it had left. I was having shoulder pain. It was very hard to lift my arm. Elisha prayed for my shoulder a few times, and some of the pain went away. The next day, I noticed the difference. The pain lessened until it was no more. I was able to lift my arm all the way up to the sky. I was so excited because I hadn't been able to lift my arm in over a week to date. I haven't had any problems with my arm since. To God be the glory.

Me, Renata (seated), and Mom (Deborah)
checking the length of her legs.
Michigan.

I did not know what to expect that night, and I did not know that this would be one of the last gatherings allowed for a while. COVID-19 cases were breaking out then, and we didn't know it. The news outlets soon flooded with announcements of cases into our country and Michigan. It wasn't too long before we went on lockdown. God moved in healing this night, completely blessing us together one more time.

My mother always carries a vial of oil in her purse from Jerusalem. She encouraged me to anoint everyone at the party with the oil after the prayers and before everyone departed. We had no idea what was happening, that the pandemic would affect our cities. We soon learned that this very night of the miracle party, there were other gatherings literally blocks away. There were reports of COVID breakouts and sadly, many lost their lives. I don't take it lightly that God covered us, the Holy Spirit met us, and miracles were reported.

I wonder if it is because we spent time with Him that night. We included Him and did not have any personal motives. It was truly a beautiful time, and I'm glad I was obedient to the leading of the Holy

Spirit. It is not always easy to pluck up courage to ask a room full of people if anyone has pains in their body and offer prayer. That was taking a step of faith, then God did all the rest of the work.

F.F. Bosworth stated that it is just as much God's will to heal the body as it is to heal the soul. I truly believe that having this mindset encourages my decision in asking people if I can pray for them. I want people to know that receiving Jesus in our lives is just the beginning of all the wonderful things that can be done. After salvation is a journey to wholeness in spirit, soul, and body. If there are things we are dealing with in our bodies, we must view being healed as being saved in a physical sense, just like the transformation of our souls when we give our lives to Jesus. It starts with believing.

Surely everything I saw and felt in my heart was enough for me to never doubt our God. Even if He never moved again, my heart has borne witness to the works of His mighty hand. I will forever testify to the certainty of what took place, and I write the truth, so that those who learn of it might also believe (John 19:35). I lift my voice to the father right now and say, "I believe, I believe."

SPIRITUAL LESSONS LEARNED

Just like our Father in heaven, we are spirits. Our spirit man is more real than our physical bodies. We see our physical bodies with the natural eye, so because of our human nature, we tend to gravitate to what's in front of us as reality. On my journey with the Holy Spirit, the more I sought after the supernatural, I learned some hard lessons. For example, I've prayed for people and took on their symptoms because I did not treat the sickness as an unwanted guest.

Now every spirit that I approach and pray for, I treat as if it is a person. I tell it to get out and do not touch anyone else, to report to the feet of Jesus to be dealt with as He desires. Otherwise, the contrary spirit will try to attach to someone else nearby, including me. This happened when I prayed for a lady at church decades ago and when I prayed for my husband a few years back.

The lady I prayed for was having severe back pains. We were just dismissed from a church service, and I went about greeting people customarily on my way out. When I spoke to her, she complained of pain. Without the experience I have now, I reached out and placed my hand on her back in a circular motion as we continued talking. Not even a minute later, she said, “Wow, my back is feeling better!” and she thanked me. Well to me, I didn’t feel like I did anything, but to see her pain free and smiling made me happy.

Later that evening, I was sitting at home and when I tried to get up, I couldn’t. I felt a sharp pain in my back, and it scared me. I called for my husband, who almost had to pick me up; even still, it was so painful that I went to the hospital to be checked out. They couldn’t find any issues with me. We later discovered that the lady I prayed for was completely healed of her back issue, but I took on her symptoms. We prayed until it left me. But my eyes were opened, and I learned from that moment. Spirits can transfer. Maybe this is one of the reasons 1 Timothy 5:22 says to lay hands suddenly on no man.

Another time when I experienced spirits transferring, my husband came under attack in his body. He was preparing for a large production and was to lead out in presenting music for our family ministry,

Righteous Antidote. The night before the event, his left elbow swelled up as if water had gathered. He was in a lot of pain and could not bend his arm at all. His left hand also swelled up with hives. He had never experienced this before, and it was sudden.

We both figured this could not be coincidence; this event planned for months now was a major part of the ministry that he had been doing. It seemed he was under spiritual attack. I prayed for him, I placed my hand on his elbow and commanded the swelling to leave in the name of Jesus. For all the pain to leave, in the name of Jesus. I did not, however, tell it to leave our house and not touch anyone else. Immediately as I prayed for him, we both felt the liquid drain from his elbow. He was amazed and so was I. It was not until the next morning, the morning of the event, that I woke and realized that I could not use my left arm. I took on the pain because I failed to cast that spirit/person to the feet of Jesus and command it to leave our house. I spent the entire event supporting the production work without the full functionality of my left arm. It eventually left me as I renounced it and commanded it to go over the next day. But this was a lesson well learned.

I want to encourage every reader not to be afraid of the enemy. To make sure when we pray against the forces of darkness that we do it in Jesus' name, use discernment, and ask the Holy Spirit for knowledge on what's going on around you. Just like Mark 6:13, "*They cast out many demons and anointed many sick people with oil and healed them.*" We must know who we are and proceed in what Jesus taught us to do, do it in His name and forbid everything contrary from touching anyone else.

Jesus dealt with the demons in people, not the people. Mark 1:23 shows how suddenly in a meeting a demon-possessed man screamed out. Then verse 25 states that Jesus rebuked him (the demon) and expelled the demon from the man. Jesus did not kick the man out of the synagogue. This was a regular occurrence with Jesus. He was ready, not taken aback by disturbances. Dealing with these spiritual beings was a part of His total ministry. I feel that we, as believers, must stay alert, prayed up, and ready to operate from Jesus' example. Learn these lessons like I did and keep going; take authority.

EVEN IF YOU DON'T SEE IT

I don't pretend to know it all. All I can confirm is that it is the power of God. First Corinthians 13:9 says it best, that right now we know in part, but one day we will know fully, even as we are known fully by God. But right now, can we ever truly get our carnal mind (our flesh) to line up to the truth? No, we can't. The scriptures say in Romans 8:7, "*The carnal mind is at enmity (hostile) against God. It is not subject to the law of God.*" No matter how hard we try to train it, it will never cooperate. So instead of trying to fix our brains, we must learn to just shut it off. Renew our spiritual minds according to Romans 12:2. To be inwardly transformed by the Holy Spirit. It is a total reformation of how to think. We must trust that process and have complete faith in God, not faith in what is seen with the natural eye. 2 Corinthians 4:18 says, "*As we look not to the things that are seen but to the things that are unseen. For the things that are seen are transient, but the things that are unseen are eternal.*" It's as simple as getting out of our own head and saying, "Father, what would You like for me to see and say?"

One day, one of my coworkers, a very nice lady, was sitting close by, leaning back in her chair. It was a bit unusual how she was sitting, so I asked if she was okay. She said that her back was hurting her so bad and that ever since she'd been in a car accident years ago, she's always been hurting with migraines as well. When someone offers to tell me so openly of their pain and issues, I immediately take it as an invitation to pray. Before I knew it, I was offering to pray for her. She gladly accepted.

I told her to continue to sit in the chair, and I measured the length of her feet. One of her heels seemed longer than the other, so I prayed and asked Jesus to level that out for her and remove all the pain from her body. I commanded all the pain in her body to report to Jesus' feet. I told her to test it out. She did and couldn't believe that it felt better. I don't think she was a believer before this experience. But now her eyes have been open to the truth. That our Jesus heals. Miracles can break out in all of our workplaces; all it takes is one of us to step out in faith because we believe.

PRAYER AND ACTIVATION:

Let's stand in agreement now for boldness and courage to step out in faith, to be a light for Jesus, and express His Kingdom realties everywhere we go. To be excited and honored to serve Jesus. Let's talk to the Father together:

Dear Heavenly Father,

We commit ourselves to You, to be used by You to represent Your Kingdom. We are excited about it and are so honored to help build Your Kingdom here on earth.
Forgive us for every moment we gave in to man-fearing spirits. This is nothing but a tool used by the enemy to limit our supernatural journey with our beloved Holy Spirit. You have not given us the spirit of fear, but of power and love and a sound mind. Forgive us for every sin as we forgive those who have sinned against us.
We lay every weight at Your feet right now and commit our walk solely to You. We want to make Jesus more famous. Not that You need us at all to do that, but it pleases You, our dear Father, to use us for Your glory.
We confess now that we are ambassadors for Christ. That we have authority to be representatives of the government of heaven. That we are on assignment to fulfill Mark 16:15-18, "everywhere we go, let Your light be seen."
We are not foreigners of heaven. We are foreigners on earth. We are protected and fully equipped with the gospel and testimonies of our Jesus. If we stay on assignment, we are covered and in alignment so that the traps of the enemy will not work.
We commit to seeking the heart and mind of Jesus. We walk according

to Galatians 2:20, crucified with Christ, yet living. Being transformed into the image of Christ according to 2 Corinthians 3:18. Instead of just reading of all the miracles of Jesus, we are walking miracles, doing the greater works that Jesus spoke of as He ascended. That our lives will be full of demonstrations of Your hand.

We believe, decree, and declare it now in Jesus' name. Amen

Chapter Four

APRIL MIRACLES

"If you cling to your life, you will lose it, and if you let your life go, you will save it." Luke 17:33

THERE WERE SO MANY cases of COVID-19 surfacing, many jobs, including mine, had issued a work-from-home order. Same for the kids in schools. So much political upheaval, as well as social and racial injustices were occurring. I've never seen anything like this before. I can only think about what Jesus said in Matthew 24, signs that alert us of His soon return and the end of the world. Verse 7 says, "*Nation will go to war against nation, and kingdom against kingdom.*" "Nation" doesn't just mean countries against countries. It means nation as in nationalities, and we've been seeing that for a very long time. There will be famines and earthquakes in many parts of the world. While all this is happening, God is yet showing us that He is with us. His Word is true, as said in Hebrew 13:5, "*I will never leave you nor forsake you*". I truly feel this is the reason the Holy Spirit led me to share testimonies. In the middle of this pandemic, many are experiencing a touch from God either through healing or deliverances. I think we can miss out on what He's doing if we focus only on what's happening in the news. We have to let go of our lives and surrender our time and prayers for the edification of others. This is true life (Luke 17:33).

FREE FOOD AND PRAYERS

Our family ministry, Righteous Antidote, has partnered with churches for local food drives to distribute throughout our community. Staying at home due to the lockdown for some meant no pay. This was truly a difficult time for many. In the United States and countries like India, even continents like Africa, the stay-at-home order was implemented and all access to food and work had stopped. God sent finances to us so that we could share it with families and ministries locally and globally. Glory to our God for provisions. We set a schedule to go pick up food crates weekly to pass out in our neighborhood and cities nearby. We drove up and down the streets, and if we saw people outside, we stopped and asked if they could use some fresh food. Some were glad to receive it, some were in tears and asked if they could take some for their extended families, and there were a few who didn't need it at all. We just continued to drive around and drop off boxes until they were all gone. While giving food, we also offered prayers. Miracles started to happen, and many were encouraged and thankful.

My husband (Dameon) picking up crates of food to pass out. Michigan.

DELIVERANCE PRAYER

Righteous Antidote has also been blessed to feed families in other countries. This is how we met Christy from Nigeria. Although she is in Nigeria and we are in the United States, she has been connected to us for years and has become like family. And it was not until the pandemic that she shared with us the troubling reality of what was really happening in her country due to lockdowns. She gave me permission to share her story and how God moved on her behalf.

Her parents are in their senior years and her father's health has not been the best. She also has younger siblings, so she felt the weight of trying to provide for the home. In some areas, not all, if men outside of the home were to help them, they require sexual favors in return. In a desperate attempt to provide, many women have been tempted to go that route. Christy gave her life to God, though, and wanted nothing to do with that life anymore. We vowed to send funds to help her family and we will continue to do so.

Christy began praying and really seeking God. We shared with her scriptures and words of knowledge. She noticed a pattern. The more she prayed with us, the more she was tormented by an evil presence. At night, when she went to bed, a demon would come to her room and rape her until morning. (These are her words.) It is so troubling, the harsh reality is that many are tormented by evil spirits in ways they never share. The more she prayed, the more violent the demon treated her. She also had dreams of someone chasing her with a knife to kill her. She was so afraid and never wanted to pray again.

She shared all these details with me in a desperate attempt to get an understanding and seek help. I immediately thought of a "spirit spouse." Also known as incubus and succubus, they are spirits that seek to sleep with a person while they are sleeping. I prayed and sought the Holy Spirit on how to help her. I wanted to pray with her over the phone, but the only way we could pray together was by voice clips because of the distance and weak signal. This was before I learned of WhatsApp, but as far as I know, she was not aware of it either. We only spoke through Facebook, and the signal was so bad through Messenger. So, I took my phone, recorded voice clips, and emailed it to her. I instructed her to pray with the recording and to believe.

Many aren't aware of the different dark spirits that can torment, like spirit husbands or spirit wives. These spirits are not from God. God only permits and ordains humans to marry. Hebrews 13:4 says, "*Give honor to marriage, and remain faithful to one another in marriage. God will surely judge people who are immoral and those who commit adultery.*" This is not true life. Satan always does the opposite of what

God purposes for us. He uses it for evil. His whole agenda is to steal, kill, and destroy (John 10:10), to hinder our destiny in Jesus.

A "spirit spouse" or "soul tie" can destroy a marriage. It is a spirit that literally lies in the middle of a husband and a wife, causing them to come together no longer, to not desire one another. It also drives away potential spouses, so that a single person will remain single and subject to the dark spirit. I've seen people engaged several times but for some reason, things go wrong and it is like there is a force to stay unmarried. This could be caused by the spirit spouse. It is all spiritual warfare and must be dealt with spiritually.

Ephesians 6:12 says, "*For we are not fighting against flesh-and-blood enemies, but against evil rulers and authorities of the unseen world, against mighty powers in this dark world, and against evil spirits in the heavenly places.*"

These spirits are not seen with the natural eye. But through the Word of God, we have the tools to defeat the enemy. Christians give their lives to God and can still be tormented by the devil. If this is happening to you, it is your time to be free. If you've come into agreement with darkness, knowingly or unknowingly, God wants to free you now.

There are several ways that a "spirit spouse" or "soul tie" can enter our bodies. To name a few, molestation, fully by penetration or fondling by a child or an adult—basically when a child discovered the knowledge of sex. Physically raped, raped in dreams, premarital sex—fornication (having sex with someone who is not your husband), sexual lust, masturbation, pornography, idolatry in family lineage, or witchcraft in our family lineages. It is important to know that if this is happening in your dreams, it is an evil spirit, no matter how it disguises itself, appearing as a loved one, or an ex. Don't be deceived.

If it is hard to determine the root of how this spirit connected or entered, it is always wise to pray and ask the Holy Spirit to bring it back to memory, everything He wants exposed. Sometimes if things are tragic, painful, or embarrassing, we tend to try and block it from our minds and forget about it, but those very things we can give to Jesus so He can set us free. If you're feeling uneasiness while reading this now, just say out loud, "Your time is up, spirit of darkness. You've been exposed by Jesus."

Say the prayer below out loud from your heart. If you feel any form of uneasiness or agitation, just know it is the evil spirit leaving. Command it to the feet of Jesus immediately. Think of a thief or stranger that breaks into your house. Would you be calm, quiet, and polite? Or will you command that person to leave your house? I would shout, "Get Out NOW! In the name of Jesus!" This is the prayer that I sent to Christy.

PRAYER FOR DELIVERANCE FROM SPIRIT SPOUSE AND SOUL TIES

"Dear Heavenly Father,

I ***RECOGNIZE*** *there is a spirit that is assigned to torment me. Please forgive me for coming into agreement with every contrary spirit in Jesus' name. I come as humbly as I know how,* ***REPENTING****, asking for forgiveness and releasing those I've held grudges, unforgiveness, and resentment towards.*

Mark 11:25-26 says, "And whenever you stand praying, if you have anything against anyone, forgive him, that your Father in heaven may also forgive you your trespasses. But if you do not forgive, neither will your Father in heaven forgive your trespasses." *So, I choose to lay everything at the feet of Jesus now.*

I join in agreement according to Matthew 18:20, which says, "For where two or three are gathered together in My name (Jesus), I am there in the midst of them."

Your word also says in Matthew 18:18, "Whatever you bind on earth will be bound in heaven, and whatever you loose on earth will be loosed in heaven."

Because of this word, Father, now in the name of Jesus, I ***RENOUNCE*** *every spirit spouse, soul tie, incubus and succubus spirits. Every familiar, unclean, and perverted spirit, I renounce you in Jesus' name. I command you to be* ***REMOVED*** *from my life.*

COME OUT!

Right NOW, COME OUT of my will, COME OUT of my emotions, and COME OUT of my body!

Now in the name of Jesus, spirit spouse, I command you to COME OUT!

In the name of Jesus, every spirit that is not from God, every spirit that is not from the Holy Spirit, I cast you at the feet of Jesus, to be dealt with as He desires. Through the authority of Jesus Christ, I expel you from my body and to the feet of Jesus.

I repent, Father, of every sin that I've committed, sexually, mentally, emotionally, I'm sorry for coming into agreement with it and now command it to go, I am no longer in agreement with any darkness. And I will not operate in sin anymore. I bind every spirit that is not from heaven.

Spirit spouse, pack your bags, load up all your stuff, and go.

Now go to a door of your house and open the door, once the door is open, yell,

Get OUT IN THE NAME OF JESUS! I cut you with divine scissors, any connection from my family's bloodline, any contrary spirit that traveled through the umbilical cord from the womb, every spirit of witchcraft, idolatry, I severe your head right now.

Every spirit of a snake COME OUT! Every spirit of a jezebel COME OUT! Marine Spirits COME OUT! Spirits from the water, COME OUT! GET OUT IN THE NAME OF JESUS! I am covered by the blood of Jesus.

I declare my home, my family, my mind, and my life to be controlled only by the Holy Spirit. The blood of Jesus is poured over my house. The blood of Jesus breaks every contract that the enemy has used to torment me. It is disconnected and pronounced null and void.

Heavenly Father, I ask now that you ***REFILL*** *me from the inside out with Your Spirit. Send heavenly angels to war on my behalf. Leave no place in me empty. Every compartment within me. Holy Spirit BURN!*

Holy Spirit, BURN! BURN! BURN!

PURIFY! BURN! BURN! BURN!

PURIFY Me from the inside out!

A CLEAN SWEEP! A CLEAN FLUSH!

Everything that should not be is OUT! OUT! OUT!

IN THE NAME OF JESUS! JESUS! JESUS! JESUS! JESUS!

Consume my body with FIRE! FIRE! FIRE!

From the crown of my head to the sole of my feet, I declare freedom now, and whom the son sets free is free indeed. Every spirit of lust, every spirit of uncleanliness, every spirit of darkness, it stops with me in the name of Jesus.

Now I take a deep breath in of the Holy Spirit (breath in deep) *and release every single bit of darkness, again* (breath in deep) *I release all else.*

Holy Spirit take place where the darkness used to reside. My body is the temple of the Holy Spirit. Every door of the devil is now closed, and only the door of Jesus is opened. I decree and declare it so in Jesus' name.

Amen and Amen!

SATURDAY, APRIL 18, 2020

I asked Christy to let me know how it went when she gave the recorded prayer a try. She was afraid to pray at first but was bold enough to pray it out loud. She messaged me soon after in shock because of what she experienced. She said she had not felt anything like that before. She said she felt as if I were standing right in front of her, and she could hardly stand straight because something supernatural began to happen. A shaking and vibration in her stomach, then a force came out of her as she commanded the spirit spouse to leave.

I thought, wow, that's our Jesus. I'm in the United States and she's in Africa, but there is no distance in the Spirit. God is omnipresent, omniscient, omnipotent, always present, in all places, with all power. God's Word is laced with who He is and all we are required to do is stand in faith and pray it over our lives.

God addressed her case because she believed, standing in agreement and being bold to take authority and reject the devil. I'm so happy and thankful that God loves us and has given us power to fight against the adversary. That no matter what we've been through, He waits for us; He is the door to freedom, love, and wholeness. My heart is overjoyed for her and every reader who experiences the same deliverance she has.

From this moment on, the torment ended and has not returned. Here is a testimony that she also gave me permission to share.

Testimony

I am from Nigeria. Before I met Elisha, I was battling with spirit spouse and nightmares to the extent I became afraid to pray. The more I prayed, the more severe the attack. So, I stop praying because I became so scared. But after meeting mama (as I call her), I told her what I was going through. She sent a prayer to me through voice clips. So, I summoned courage to pray. Glory to God! As I was praying, I had a strange sound and a shaking in my stomach, and something jumped out of my body. From that day, I've had no more harassments by the spirit spouse and no more nightmares. Hallelujah! Glory to God!
Christy. Nigeria.

FREEDOM THROUGH JESUS

To be completely free through Jesus, we must first confess according to Romans 10:9-10, "*If you openly declare that Jesus is Lord and believe in your heart that God raised him from the dead, you will be saved. For it is by believing in your heart that you are made right with God, and it is by openly declaring your faith that you are saved.*" Then we humble ourselves and confess all the wrongs that we've done, asking for forgiveness, and agreeing to live for Christ the best we know how.

Next, we must forgive others. This can be very hard to do, but with the help of God, it is possible. I've noticed most people that I pray for who need deliverance and healing were holding a grudge, resentment, or unforgiveness in their heart toward someone else. Satan uses unforgiveness as a door and access point to attack in many ways. Unforgiveness can destroy a person like an incurable cancer. It is so important to close that door. I can't say it enough.

Ephesians 4:31 says, "*Let all bitterness and wrath and anger and clamor* [perpetual animosity, resentment, strife, fault-finding] *and slander be put away from you, along with every kind of malice* [all spitefulness, verbal abuse, malevolence]. *Be kind and helpful to one another, tender-hearted* [compassionate, understanding], *forgiving one another* [readily and freely], *just as God in Christ also forgave you*."

We can be believers and still struggle with spirits. As long as we live in a natural body, we will have to be on guard and keep the whole armor of God on so that we can stand against the wiles of the devil. As soon as we recognize which schemes and plots Satan has been using against us, we must immediately close that door. Only open the door of Jesus and live a free and prosperous life.

Below are a few scriptures that helped me on my journey to forgiveness. I struggled with letting go of some hurts from the past, and I wanted to ask God to forgive me for holding on to it. One by one, I said these scriptures out loud. For every person that I could think of, I wrote their names down, and I gave it to Jesus. If I had any bitterness, resentment, grudge, or unforgiveness at all toward them, I wanted it to stop.

I tore up that list of names and threw it in the garbage as a symbol of unforgiveness towards them being torn from me and casted away, never to wrestle with it again. I had to declare forgiveness in my life and that I'm not in agreement with hurt from the past.

Satan is not at all concerned with our past. He has moved on to try to set new traps for the future. He uses hurt people, people who are tormented by their own limitations, issues, or traumas. Satan caused the problem, or planted the seed, he does his dirt and then moves on. But it takes more work for us sometimes to let go, to not get stuck in the past, because we are human and have feelings.

We must recognize unforgiveness for what it is: it is a torturing tool that Satan uses. Many are tortured in their minds, their bodies with sickness or limited in life because they can't seem to move forward. Let's make sure all is forgiven and give it to Jesus now. It's a choice to let go of anger, resentment, bitterness, hatred, and grudges. It is not about an emotion. It is a decision of the will. Once your mind is made up, then you can verbally say out loud that you choose to forgive this person or that person of all the wrong that happened. Once this is done, there is a spiritual release, a supernatural release. Here are some scriptures that helped me with forgiveness.

- Mark 11:25
    - "But when you are praying, first forgive anyone you are holding a grudge against, so that your Father in heaven will forgive your sins, too."
- Matthew 6:14-15

    - "For if you forgive men their trespasses, your heavenly Father will also forgive you. But if you do not forgive men their trespasses, neither will your Father forgive your trespasses."

- 1 John 1:9
    - "But if we confess our sins to him, he is faithful and just to forgive us our sins and to cleanse us from all wickedness."

- Hebrews 8:12
    - "And I will forgive their wickedness, and I will never again remember their sins."

- Proverbs 10:12
    - "Hatred stirs up quarrels, but love makes up for all offenses."

- Psalms 103:3
    - "He forgives all my sins and heals all my diseases."

- Psalms 66:18
    - "If I had not confessed the sin in my heart, the Lord would not have listened."

HEALING FROM HEART FAILURE

My husband and I stood in prayer with a lady named Cassandra, a woman he used to work with. Really, it was set up by God. She needed prayer and had tried to reach out months before, but we never knew about it. I feel this is no coincidence. God knows our hearts, and when we are truly ready to receive healing and deliverance. My husband called her to discuss work, but the Holy Spirit led him to just listen to her. She thought he was calling about her sickness, but we were unaware of her condition.

She shared what she was facing, and it was life threatening. My husband and I immediately began praying for her. I started by asking the Holy Spirit to reveal the root of the cause for her sickness. While praying this, my husband received a word of knowledge almost immediately and asked me to stop praying. He's never done that before, I stopped, and we began to listen to what the Holy Spirit revealed.

He told Cassandra there is someone she needed to forgive, that unforgiveness has been used as a gateway for this sickness. Whatever she had to do, whomever she had to forgive, to do it swiftly. To my surprise, she knew exactly what he was talking about and agreed. She got off the phone with us and did what was in her heart to do to let go of unforgiveness. That was the shortest prayer call I'd ever been on. But it is so wonderful, God didn't want us to pray amiss. God revealed it, she humbled herself, released it, and the rest is history.

What heart failure? The devil thought he would take her life prematurely, but she is still alive and well today. She needed a new heart, and she got one through her submission to Jesus. She celebrates and gives God glory for saving her. I'm thankful for her obedience and the example she has set in being submissive to the Word of God.

Whenever we talk, we remember what a merciful and beautiful God we serve. How her healing began the day she chose to walk in forgiveness. Our prayer is that if you or someone you know is suffering from heart failure, that you also will be healed as Cassandra was in the name of Jesus. That the root of bitterness and unforgiveness will be broken off. That Jesus will get the glory and that every hidden agenda of the devil will be exposed. God forgives us of our iniquities if we forgive others, and He heals our diseases. Glory to Jesus forever! I asked for permission to share her testimony and she was glad to. Here are her words.

Testimony

On April 29, 2017, I was diagnosed with congestive heart failure. Sometime later, I got a call from Dameon regarding some work. I thought he was calling about my health, of which he had no idea about it. I then gave him my diagnosis. He said, 'Well, we got to pray.' He then called for Elisha to join the conversation. While she was praying, Dameon said, 'Stop, there's some-

one that you [me] *must first forgive.' He asked if I knew who or what he was talking about and that I couldn't let the sun go down without fixing the situation. He also stated that my illness was not unto death, but I had to forgive that day! I immediately called the person, met with them that day, explained my reason for needing to see them, and I said, 'I forgive you!' They were so confused, but I felt so much better! I had been told I needed a heart transplant. However, on January 4, 2018, I was taken off the transplant list and God has kept me to this very day with my own heart beating on time! God is so faithful, and His Word is true! I owe Him everything! Dameon and Elisha I do believe were very instrumental in my healing, and I will never forget. I love you both forever!*
Cassandra. Michigan.

HIS SPIRIT WITHIN

It is so amazing to know the truth that as soon as we come into relationship with Jesus, supernatural things begin to happen. In April, in the United States, we celebrate the death, burial, and resurrection of Jesus. I would be remiss not to note the incredible thing that Jesus did. He knew when and how He was going to be crucified for us. He told the disciples of these plans and that it would be good for Him to go. John 16:7 says, "*Nevertheless I tell you the truth. It is to your advantage that I go away.*"

This must have been very confusing for the disciples, and I imagine exceedingly difficult to accept. I would not want to be parted from Jesus after walking side by side with Him either. Experiencing unimaginable love, healing, miracles, and hope for the world. My eyes being opened to Kingdom realities for the first time. But Jesus explained that He had to experience death, burial, and resurrection for the sins of the world, that we could all have access to the Father through Him. And Jesus explained that when He departs, He would send us a helper. "*...for if I do not go away, the Helper will not come to you; but if I depart, I will send Him to you.*" Basically, this means that Jesus would send the Holy Spirit, the power of God, so we would never be alone. He would be with us to show us all things. We would be able to walk as Jesus walked because we are redeemed.

Whenever we pray in the name of Jesus, with the power of the Holy Spirit that resides in us as believers (we must receive Jesus first and be a believer to receive the gift of the Holy Spirit), wonderful things are bound to happen. We can stand in agreement with anyone else who is calling on the name of Jesus, testify of what Jesus has done, that He was wounded for us, bruised for us, and by His stripes, we are healed.

WEDNESDAY, APRIL 29, 2020

No matter what issues come in life, our Jesus can take care of it. This is what I told a married couple, David and Alexia. My husband and I have known David since forever it seems! We were so happy to celebrate him and his beautiful wife's (Alexia) union. They reached out for prayer because Alexia had been suffering from endometriosis, which is when pain is caused by abnormal tissues that form in and outside of the reproductive organs.

The Holy Spirit reminded me of when I was eighteen years old. A doctor diagnosed me with having fibroid tumors. Then I learned that it ran in my family. As I did my research, I learned that up to seventy percent of women have fibroids. They are not always painful, but it is very common. I still didn't like that diagnosis. I was not suffering with pains from it, but I knew the doctor told me I had some and I know women who were having a rough time with it. Some had no other option but to have a hysterectomy.

I told Alexia I had fibroids for two years. The fibroids didn't go away because I decided that I didn't like the idea of it. When I had my encounter with the Holy Spirit in 2000, that's when I changed my confession. I started speaking healing over myself. I didn't feel a change, nor did I see it. It wasn't time for my annual appointment with the OBGYN yet. I didn't know what God would do, but I knew He was able. I really did not come into agreement with that diagnosis, even before I knew how powerful a mindset can be.

The scriptures say in Proverbs 23:7, "*For as he thinks in his heart, so is he.*" This means the decisions, actions, and directions we take stem from what's in our innermost being, our hearts and in our minds. At first, I just ignored the diagnosis, but when I was filled with the Holy Spirit, I addressed how I felt about it. There are scriptures that I would come across that made it difficult for me to come into agreement with a diagnosis. That I'm created in His image and mere thoughts that I have are so powerful that it can become a physical reality. That I need to change my mind (Romans 12:2), to guard my thoughts (Philippians 4:7), and to know the thoughts that God has towards me (Jeremiah 29:11). And as a man thinks in his heart, so is he (Proverbs 23:7).

After meditating on these, I started praying and canceling every bloodline issue from both my father's and mother's sides. I asked God to go back as far as needed, all the way back to Adam and Eve. I commanded any issues that ran in the family to be broken. Health issues, hidden spiritual blockages, familiar spirits, uncleanliness, limitations, etc. I said out loud, "I break it, disallow it, dispossess it from my family in the name of Jesus."

I had my annual checkup with a new OBGYN after I got married and moved to another city. Over time, I almost forgot about the diagnosis because there was no pain, so I went on as though nothing was there. But during my annual checkup, we were about to wrap things up, and I remembered the diagnosis from the other doctor, so I asked my new OBGYN to check the status of the fibroids. That I was told that I had them two years ago. She looked at me puzzled and said she didn't see anything. But she offered to check once more to confirm.

She checked and told me that there was nothing, no fibroids at all. I asked her if she was sure, and she confirmed that nothing was there. I've been sharing my testimony ever since. God is so good!

Three children later, and over two decades since that diagnosis, I have never had a fibroid surface. Glory to God!

I told Alexia the same God that did that for me can remove endometriosis. This is nothing for our God to manage. She was very encouraged by my story. And although she had a mass (6 cm x 4 cm) plaguing her, we prayed together for healing. I didn't touch her; we were over the phone. That's how you know it is God.

Normally this size mass would require surgery, but God worked a miracle for her. We discussed scriptures on healing and asked God for forgiveness if she'd come into agreement with this or any other issue. Laying everything at the feet of Jesus. Her and her husband were soon to go to the doctors to have an updated examination, surgery would have been the next thing on the agenda, but they chose to stand in agreement with our Chief Physician and what He wanted to do about it. They gave me permission to share the results and how powerful our God moved on their behalf.

I'm so excited for them and standing in agreement with them for every prayer and blessing to flow in Jesus' name. I am smiling now because as I'm writing this, they informed us of the baby that's on the way. The very thing that they were concerned about is annihilated. We serve a defy-the-odds type of God! Here is the testimony they gave me permission to share:

Testimony

Elisha is a fierce prayer warrior who has blessed my husband and I beyond belief. In January, we learned that a 6 cm x 4 cm mass was found behind my uterus and could prevent conception as well as require surgery. In April, we shared our story with Elisha. She was very empathetic and began praying for us. She also shared personal testimonies with us about conception, fertility, and demonstration of the power of

prayer. In May, we followed up with the doctors and the results came back that the large hemorrhagic mass had resolved! I truly believe it was due to Elisha praying over us and casting out the devil. Elisha makes an awesome addition to the Spirit Lifestyle community.
David and Alexia. Michigan.

PRAYER AND ACTIVATION:

We can have true life and light in Jesus. We must completely decide to give up the old ways for His ways. He loves us so much and wants us to be saved, free, healed, and delivered. If you're in agreement with that, let's talk to the Father together:

Dear Heavenly Father,

Thank You for a heart that wants to completely get rid of the old man (Ephesians 4:22-24). As I yield to You, let Your light shine through me, from the inside out (Isaiah 60:1). Let Your Truth be revealed and expose every lie of the enemy. I want to be completely free.
Turn the searchlight on me, every spirit of darkness that wants to hold me captive, burn it with Your fire (Psalms 51:10). Give me the grace to forgive and the boldness to reject every unclean spirit. Sanctify my mind through Your Word and testimony (1 Thessalonians 5:23). I want my whole being to be fully consumed in You. I want to be full proof of what Christ did for me, living a life free from the curse of sin, torment, oppression, sickness, disease, and death.
I decree and declare that I am free now and every step I take is orchestrated by You, Father (Psalms 37:23). Steps of progress, success, prosperity, and greatness. The life that I now live in this flesh, I live by the faith of the Son of God, who loved me and gave himself for me (Galatians 2:20).
I will focus on Your truth and Your light. Things that are true, honest, just, pure, and of good report. (Philippians 4:8)
In Jesus' name. Amen.

Chapter Five

MAY MIRACLES

"For the Kingdom of God is not just a lot of talk; it is living by God's power."
1 Corinthians 4:20

I PROMISED MY BELOVED Holy Spirit that I would never pass up an opportunity to share about the goodness of Jesus. Not only by talking, but by demonstrating God's power. I want to be a walking billboard of not only His healing power but also His sustaining power. Some people talk a lot about faith, but that's all they do, talk. Faith without action is pretty much just talk. It is not enough to just know the right words to say. It is not enough when the reflective power of God is not seen. We need to step out in faith to see what amazing supernatural things will happen. It is such an awesome way to display how real God is.

God truly knows the motives of our heart. He aligns us so that His purpose can be fulfilled; that's if we yield to His voice. I feel this is how I've become a volunteer Spirit Lifestyle Coach. I've officially partnered with this ministry from the United Kingdom, and now I'm coaching sessions on supernatural living every week. It was 2012 when I first came across Spirit lifestyle. I saw a video of Aliss Cresswell on Sid Roth's "It's Supernatural." The words she shared hit me like a sledgehammer.

God took me through a series of supernatural experiences over the years, but I didn't know why. I didn't know my story would help others. I didn't know God would lead people to me to use me as an instrument to help others to be healed and be set free. I would have never dreamt of having a voice for Jesus—not with what I had been through and the mistakes I've made. There is a voice inside of us all that will draw people to who God is in us. There are no coincidences. So, in my coaching sessions, I teach on how to live a Christian life by including the Holy Spirit in everything.

For example, when I model, I model after Christ, although I'm in the world doing a job, I'm not of the world. My job is to shine for Jesus in every arena. I encourage everyone in the session to remember that when we receive Jesus, our spirit connects with the Holy Spirit. We can completely yield our lives to God and see ourselves as dispensers of His Spirit. This should be the norm for us as believers: to walk according to the scriptures and to do what we read about in the book of Acts.

If we adopt this mindset, many amazing spiritual things can happen around us. It is an adventure with the Holy Spirit. He shows us what to do next. If you would have told me years ago that I would agree to be a Christian minister or a Spirit Lifestyle Coach, I probably would not have believed it because of my introverted tendencies.

With a heart to help others to draw close to Jesus, I've decided to stop limiting Him and getting in the way. I encourage others that God can use ordinary people like you and me to impact our world. We are all commissioned to do so.

TUESDAY, MAY 5, 2020

My daughter, Salah, loves to hear about the supernatural happening all around us. I wrote in Chapter 3 about her verbally saying she wanted to see a miracle and she saw one in a restaurant. As a 15-year-old in 2020, now a teenager, she has been seeking God for herself. We pray together and study the Word as a family. This night, she had an encounter. We just finished a family movie night. We watched *War Room*, which was originally a book written by Priscilla Shirer. We try to encourage our children to watch inspirational movies, movies that focus on Jesus.

When we went to bed, Salah was sleeping and felt a nudge to wake up and pray. A literal person nudging, a physical push on her body to wake her up. She turned over and thought maybe it was just her imagination, but it happened again. This time she sat up in her bed, startled. She came into my room, woke me, and told me what happened. She also told me that she felt an urgency to pray. So, I went to her room with her. I always want to stay ready for moments like these, whenever my children want to pray or need an explanation of Scripture or world events. It was around 2:00 a.m. when she woke me. I was so sleepy but pressed my way and got up to be with her.

What if it was a heavenly angel that nudged her? What if it was a demon that was trying to torment her? I went with her, and we kneeled at her bed, shoulder to shoulder. I started the prayer, humbling, submitting, asking forgiveness, and just inviting the Holy Spirit to come and fill us again. Then Salah began to pray. Salah has dealt with a spirit of fear for some time now. She was in elementary school when she started to deal with it; it was the Halloween time of year, and a teacher played a horror movie during school hours. I noticed ever since that time, she slept with her closet light on. The enemy took advantage of a moment when she was away from her parents, at school, to plant a seed of fear.

We never encourage Halloween movies at home, as we don't celebrate that day at all. Any day that promotes witches, goblins, spells, fear, darkness, demons, and death should be a red flag. Halloween is a holy day for Satanists. I never understood how Christians see nothing wrong with participating in it. I wonder if Satanists celebrate resurrection Sunday or Christmas, dressing up like angels and biblical characters? There are spirits behind everything, so we have to be mindful, careful, and open to what God shows us concerning these things.

Unfortunately, I was not aware of the movie being played at school. Of course, I had a conversation with the school, and they know now, but the door was opened. The eyes and ears of my sweet little girl were infiltrated with fear. In our home, we are careful because when I was younger, I saw and heard things that I should not have. Dark spirits can get in through many gateways. Satan is cunning and will use any door left unattended. As parents, I know we will have to answer to God for our actions one day.

Salah prayed, she repented, and I've never heard her pray with that much conviction and passion before—never. She literally was crying and rejecting the spirit of fear. Because we were kneeling on the side of the bed, our shoulders touching, I felt her every move during prayer. In an instant, during the moment of her repentance, she jerked forward as though something was yanked out of her. I opened my eyes and looked at her. Her already-passionate prayers intensified. More tears ran down her face like a pool streaming into a river. She cried out to God with all her heart. I rejoiced and just kept praying along with her. The Holy Spirit was here, and she was having a supernatural encounter that she's longed for and will never forget. Her own words from her mouth released a deliverance and freedom she never saw coming.

After a while, we woke her father and we all prayed from 2:30 a.m. to 4:30 a.m., praising and worshiping God in her room. Then she went back to bed. I noticed she went back to bed with her closet light off this time. And since that day, no more closet light. The spirit of fear is gone, and we give glory to God. Here are her words on what she experienced that night.

Testimony

"We were having a family movie night. We watched "War Room." *We went to bed late, around midnight. But when I was falling asleep, I felt someone shake me. I thought I was imagining it, so I started to doze off to sleep again. Then it happened again. Someone shook me and woke me up. I felt it was God, so I immediately went into my mother's room and asked her to pray with me. We both went in my room and when we started praying, I felt something leave me, jump out of me. I felt so fresh and new. I was telling God that I was a sinner and wanted to be saved, I was spending too much time on my phone, and I only want to worship Him. That's when I felt something leave me. So, after that, I was less fearful. I believe it was the spirit of fear that left me. We stayed up and prayed more, then we went to sleep. I am so thankful that this happened. I experienced a miracle for me personally."*

My daughter, Salah, and I. Michigan.

WISDOM IS LIKE JEWELS ON A NECKLACE

I continued studying scriptures, looking into the cause and effects of deliverances, healings, and miracles. How some people are set free immediately and some gradually, and some not at all. God knows when we are ready to be healed with the truth embedded in our hearts.

Proverbs 4:20-22 says, "*My child pay attention to what I say. Listen carefully to my words. Don't lose sight of them. Let them penetrate deep into your heart, for they bring life to those who find them, and healing to their whole body.*"

I thought to myself, could this be the formula for receiving all God has for us? The seriousness of taking heed to God's Word and not allowing it to fade away or to be watered down. Meditating on it every day until it becomes a part of us. Reading it, praying it, and singing it until we believe it. It is a choice to believe God can work miracles, to believe that our current circumstances don't need to be our reality. In John 20:29, Jesus said some believed because they saw Him but blessed are those who believe and have not seen Him. This is what Jesus told Timothy when He appeared to the disciples after He rose from the dead. I'm telling you that when you're backed up against a wall, if you change your thinking and confession, you're going to have so much peace and the good thoughts you're having will start to build into outward manifestations.

We need to have faith and believe before we see the breakthrough. The Word literally works for us; it is activated when we believe. Unfortunately, if we think "doom" and that God is not near, those thoughts can build and feel like reality also. Our hearts and our feelings dictate how we will live. The summation of our words becomes our life. So how much more important is it that we grab—better yet, that we get a bulldog hold—on what God is saying and don't lose sight of it.

This requires trust, especially if we've tried everything else. When we investigate and look back at every moment when God showed up, nothing is coincidence—even the times when we didn't recognize it was God. He wants us to trust Him. He wants us not to be impressed with our own wisdom, but instead, fear the Lord and turn away from all evil according to Proverbs 3:7. Verse 8 says, "*Then you will have healing for your body and strength for your bones.*" It is the wisdom of God and the spirit of discernment that comes from Him. Verse 22 says, "*For they will refresh your soul. They are like jewels on a necklace.*"

This is the type of refreshing I want daily. To wear my jewels daily, to see His hand in all things, and to see His demonstration of power. To be healed overall, spiritually, mentally, emotionally, and physically.

WEDNESDAY, MAY 13, 2020

I received a call from a friend who lives in Oklahoma. We were chatting and just catching up. We always talk about the goodness of Jesus in our lives. She shared how she had been in pain lately, suffering with her digestive system. Not knowing what the issue was, she was feeling constant stomach pains and believed she had some inflammation in her intestines. She saw blood in her stool every time she went to the restroom, which was scary.

She was having work issues also, which we discussed earlier. Some coworkers had been giving her a tough time, and it was weighing heavy on her. We stood in agreement to pray for those coworkers and to forgive them of their actions. We also prayed for complete healing for her body. I envisioned very squeaky-clean intestines as we were praying. I spoke a creative miracle over her. That a new set of intestines would be placed in her body, out with the old, in with the new. Right after the prayer, I asked her if she was feeling anything. She said that she felt no pain. I asked her to test it out by pressing on her abdomen and moving about, but she felt nothing. That's our wonderful Jesus.

I called her back the next day to follow up and see how she was feeling. She said she went to the restroom and there was no blood in the stool surprisingly. She was so relieved and excited as she praised God. She said her stomach felt so much better. She felt a little twisting as things were passing, but now altogether better. Satan will try to convince us that we are not healed, to believe in symptoms, to believe in what we are feeling in our bodies. We have to remember to stand in agreement with what God says concerning our bodies and not what's right in front of our eyes. In everything we need wisdom, or we will agree with what we believe to be our reality.

The first part of Hosea 4:6 says, "*My people are being destroyed because they don't know me...*" The only way that we can truly know what the Father is like is to have a relationship with Him. Having knowledge about him is not enough; we must go deeper and really believe in Him. Then we will see just how much we are loved.

TEA AND PRAYER PARTY

I shared these sentiments with some ladies at a tea and prayer party. The news of the pandemic was really starting to circulate, and the numbers were rising. Masks were mandatory for our county and using hand sanitizer was encouraged. The "Tea and Prayer" party was put together by three biological sisters. They invited me and felt strongly that God wanted to do more in them. We agreed we would meet in one mutual place. I told them I would wear a mask to keep them comfortable, and we would share together. One of the sisters had been having health issues and wanted us to stand in agreement for her. I thought this would be a great idea. So, we had some tea and sat around the living room floor of one of the sister's houses. God met us there and amazing things transpired.

SATURDAY, MAY 16, 2020

As we sat and shared, I was led to tell these sisters how God blessed my relationship with my mom. How I was holding unforgiveness in my heart, how I carried resentment, how the enemy wanted me to die with a lie, thinking I wasn't loved.

I told them how I spoke to my mother and apologized for allowing the enemy to convince me to hold on to that lie for so many years. God blessed me and my mother with an unbreakable relationship. I remember the day I shared my heart with my mother, she was shocked to learn of what I had been carrying. She shared her heart with me, we prayed together, we laughed, we cried, and prayed some more. If Satan can trick us into believing a lie, he can block and postpone our progress. I can honestly say that apologizing and letting go of the lie was when the reset happened in my life. Suddenly things started to fall in line. Suddenly I was able to move forward and step into my purpose. My mother never stopped interceding for me. She even told me that while I was in her womb, she was in a terrible car accident. A car slammed into her car, and the impact was on the side where she was sitting and left black and blue bruises up and down her whole side. I flipped around in her womb, and she was afraid I would not make it. *But God!* Satan couldn't take me from her then. He tried when I grew older too, but it didn't work. God knew and saw us then and now. I encouraged these sisters to know that God sees them as well.

I found out that these sisters were dealing with the same thing—that we all have dealt with prolonged periods of time where the enemy tried to sever our relationships with our mothers. God graced us to talk through some difficult moments and traumas. We shared for hours, and I encouraged them to lay all of it at the feet of Jesus that day. Because the Holy Spirit led me on what to share with these ladies, I knew healing was taking place. Healing from lies and broken hearts, healing from toxic thinking, healing from unforgiveness.

Tears were flowing. We stayed right there to receive all that God wanted to do. Praying Mark 11:25 and breaking familiar spirits that wanted them to live in the past, to stay stuck on what transpired when they were too young to help themselves. After recommitting their lives to Jesus and repenting for the loads that they carried for so long, I then told them that anything going on in their bodies that is abnormal, Jesus can heal. They were first healed in their hearts and emotions. There was so much pain, but they gave it to Jesus. Satan can no longer use unforgiveness to cause attacks once we decide to close that door.

It turned out that one of the sisters named Nel (name adjusted for her privacy) had a bad shoulder. She could not lift it up, and it stayed in constant pain. If she lifted it up, it would pop out of the socket, causing more excruciating pain. Her doctor was planning to set up a surgery for her to repair her torn rotator cuff. As we sat on the floor with our legs folded, I asked her if she wanted prayer for her shoulder. She's tried everything but prayer up until that point.

Why not give it to Jesus to see if anything happens?

She said "Sure," so I placed my hand on her shoulder and released the healing power of Jesus. Decreeing that the joints, muscles, tissues, be restored in Jesus' name. I commanded her shoulder to be completely healed and the pain to get out right now. She looked at me and I just looked at her wondering if she felt anything. I asked her if she could test it out, but she said she didn't want to because it is painful when it pops out. I wondered how we would be able to tell if her shoulder was healed. She didn't feel anything. I was going to say, "I guess nothing means there is no pain present, so this nothing could be a good thing." But then I believe she grabbed a hold of faith. She squinted her eyes and slowly started to lift her arm.

She was expecting the pain and the part where something pops out and hurts her. But that didn't happen. Her eyes got big, and she lifted her arm all the way up. She was shocked. Her sisters were shocked, and *I* was shocked! Yes, although God moves in miracles every day all over the world, there's nothing that can prepare us for the awesomeness of experiencing it right before our eyes.

One of her sisters screamed out, "She couldn't do that before! She couldn't do that before!"

I turned to her and asked if that was true, and she said that it was true. We were extremely excited. While she had her arms lifted, I managed to grab my phone, which was on the floor next to me, and I asked her for permission to take a picture of this beautiful moment. After taking her picture, she said, "Wow, I didn't think any of this was for me."

You see, she wasn't living for Jesus currently, but our heavenly Father was always right there waiting on her with open arms. This is one of the ways Satan tries to keep people from God; I've noticed it time and time again. He plants the lie in people's minds that God is somehow angry at them, doesn't want to help them, condemning them. Everywhere we read of Jesus praying for people, He was always moved with compassion. He didn't ask if the person was living right according to His standards. He just prayed and after they were healed, He would tell them to go and sin no more. Sinning no more would be the way to stay healed and free. Jesus teaches us so well how to minister His love to our world. Walking with Him is how we are discipled and learn to live according to His word.

John 3:16 says that God loves the world so much that He gave us Jesus so that we can have reconciliation. We even see during Jesus' ministry that He went and spent time with those who didn't believe, with those the Pharisees would call sinners. The Pharisees were so self-righteous that they were too proud to show empathy and love. But God is love, and Jesus said in Luke 5:31-32 that it is not the healthy that need a doctor but those who are sick.

God sent Jesus to save a sin-sick world. God is so merciful and kind, He's chasing after each one of us. He's always speaking to us. What better way to get someone's attention than with a miracle? It's brilliant. I know when I first saw a miracle, my life was never the same. I could never doubt the existence of God, and I grew even more intrigued with Him. He healed Natalie's shoulder to show her how much He loves her. We prayed prayers to surrender to Jesus this day. What He did for her will forever be etched in our minds. I cried happy tears and was overwhelmed at His love. See the picture she shared and the testimony.

Testimony

Elisha came to have prayer with my family. We talked about being estranged from our mothers and she shared her testimony on how God blessed her relationship with her mom. It was what I needed to hear so I could forgive. We then prayed—she asked if anyone needed to be healed in their body and ended up praying for my torn shoulder. I was going to need surgery to repair it. I couldn't lift my arm up without my shoulder popping out the socket, which is very painful. But after she prayed, she asked me to test it out. I was leery to lift my arm up, but I did as she asked, and there was no pain or popping out of the socket. I couldn't do that before. I was completely shocked. Wasn't expecting that at all. I didn't know that Jesus would want to heal me, but now I know the truth.
Nel. Michigan.

We were so excited and hyped up, I told the sisters that Jesus was right there with us. That whatever they needed to just ask.

I turned to one of the other sisters named Shannon (name changed for privacy). She had a history of many things going wrong with her body, including lupus and a bad left knee due to stroke and injury. She was the reason they wanted to come together for the "Tea and Prayer." We prayed about the lupus, and I asked if I could lay my hand on her knee. I spoke to her knee in faith, not really knowing what the problem was. I told her bones and the cap at the knee to be healed and to align. Right as I was saying that her knee popped right underneath my hand. It was as though it snapped right back into place.

We simultaneously said, "Whoa!"

I asked her what she was feeling.

She said, "Something moved."

I know it felt weird for her; it felt weird for me also. I literally felt her bone against the palm of my hand. I just started to thank Jesus. She had a look in her eyes—I know this look. It was shock and awe. Like *is this really happening*. We could do nothing but continue to thank Jesus. I told her to do something she couldn't do before. She said she couldn't bend it before, couldn't stand on one leg, or hop on one leg; there was no support in that leg because of her knee injury.

She grabbed her leg and pulled her knee towards her chest. She screamed out, "I couldn't do that before!"

Shannon realized the real test would be to get up and stand on the injured leg. So, she got up from off the floor where we were sitting and hopped on that one leg and bent her knees. She went from testing her leg out to jumping hysterically with excitement and joy. We all had tears flowing at this point. It was just too beautiful an experience for words. God met us at our "Tea and Prayer" party and these sisters encountered Jesus in ways they never have before. Hallelujah!

We were all electrified from this experience. Jesus was with us from the conversation on forgiveness to the healing of these ladies' bodies. Although we were all very overwhelmed with excitement, I was glad I thought to pull out my phone to capture these moments. The expressions in the images speak for themselves.

The sister with the healed knee eventually ended up back on the floor after jumping and jumping until she was overwhelmed, crying in praise and thanksgiving. I couldn't help but think that if they had not chosen to let go and just receive the words shared on forgiveness, they would probably not have had this eye-opening touch from heaven. And it matters not where we came from, or the mistakes we've made. God is faithful and just to forgive us. He loves us so much. Just like He healed these sisters, He is healing someone who is reading this story right now. If it has not happened yet, we know that we as believers have a promise from God that suffering will one day come to an end. See the testimony below Shannon gave me to share.

Testimony

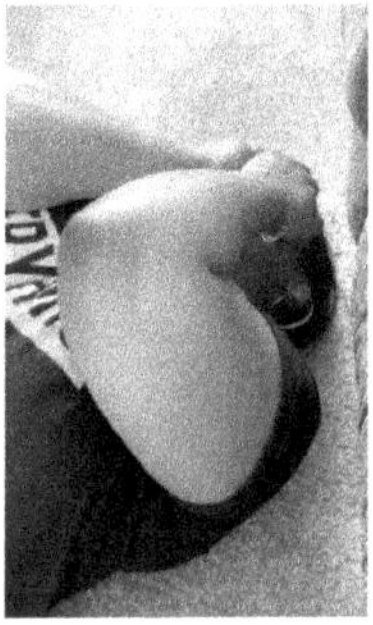

I thank God for the healing prayer that went forth. Leading up to that day, I had a stroke, been through three surgeries, chemo, and had been diagnosed with lupus among other autoimmune diseases that caused my body to be in pain. Due to a stroke on my left side and an injury, my left knee and nervous system have been enduring problems. Elisha decided that we would touch and agree in prayer that I would be healed of the pain and healed of the lupus. As she prayed, we both felt a snap in my knee. At that point, my leg began to feel better, so I decided to test the limit of my knee only to discover that I was healed. I could bend it further than I could in years, and I could stand on my left leg and balance myself with no pain. We are still praying about the lupus, and I truly believe I will have another testimony to tell that the lupus will be completely gone. Prayer changes things!
Shannon. Michigan.

PROPHETIC WORD: INHERITANCE

My first official coaching session is approaching. I've shared messages at church before, but this feels different. More intimate and allowing God to have His way, like the "Tea and Prayer" party moments. That's pretty much how the sessions I coach would go. We share about Jesus and work our way through understanding salvation. Salvation is both deliverance from sins and sickness. My mentor, Mark Yow, told me that just like these sisters that were healed, this is the season where daughters are getting their inheritance. That it is time for the women to take their rightful places.

I've loved serving in the background and watching my husband lead and wear so many hats in ministry. For over a decade, I got comfortable in a position as an intercessor. I would always say that my first ministry is my husband and children, and my home was my focus. And this is still the truth, but I had to learn to be open to the various stages that God wanted to take me in. What I did in secret, all the praying and serving others, God took me gently by the hand and said, "It is time to do it openly." I felt a tugging on my heart, and I knew it wasn't me because I would never volunteer for a position where I'd have to be in the forefront. But God called me to a place of spiritual assignments and walking in my inheritance. Heard of the daughters of Job? My mentor said this is that time. Job 42 tells of how God restored Job and everything he lost. He had ten more children. And it was revealed that "*In all the land there were found no women as beautiful as the daughters of Job, and their father granted them an INHERITANCE among their brothers.*"

To walk in the gifts of the spirit is our inheritance. To arise and shine and let His light be seen. Although it is comfortable in the background, God calls and qualifies. My husband and I have different ways and forms of doing ministry, but as we come together, it is a powerful manifestation and move of God as we yield to the Holy Spirit and lay down our own wills. This is why it is very important to remember if you are to marry, be led by God and not emotions. Our futures, families, and ministries all depend on it. The support system at home will determine the level of ministry that can be done. Ministry cannot go any further than your marriage. God does not work out of order. So doing this the right way is imperative. To answer His call and walk in places we've never been. To start a new adventure with the Holy Spirit. Only God knows all the amazing things to come. I trust Him.

SATURDAY, MAY 23, 2020

We had our first Spirit Lifestyle session this day over Zoom. Because of COVID-19, all of the churches were basically closing their doors and having meetings over the internet. I've never seen anything like it, yet here we were. I had a dream the other night of what to share during my session. I dreamed about God being the master chef, and I was a bowl/cup that He filled with all types of ingredients unique to me. All of us are unique, and God knows the recipe required to do the work He has for us. We all have so much flavor. We are the salt of the earth according to Matthew 5:13. God wants to stir up these ingredients; they are not meant to lie dormant. We are not in the earth to lay comfortably and become complacent. God wants to bring out all the flavors. That will require some stretching out of the norms of this world and operating in the norms of heaven. He knows what flavors match well with ours, so as we allow Him to add and remove things, we have to be open and obedient.

We shared on Romans 8:7 and how the carnal mind is enmity against God. Like a scrambled egg used for the recipe, our minds can sometimes feel scrambled. Sometimes on our journey, things don't look so good or feel good at all. It is like putting all our ingredients in a mixer to be blended. All the blending works together to prepare us for our main purpose. Any doubt that God is with us are lies from the enemy. We are to resist the enemy and his way of thinking according to James 4:7. No one has time for a scrambled mind at all, especially in the middle of a pandemic. We shared what this word meant to each of us and how we felt concerning it. It ended up being an encouraging right-on-time word.

I asked if anyone needed any specific prayers. I testified of the miracles that had been going on as I coached one-on-one, and moments like at the "Tea and Prayer" meeting and the Woman's Lock-In event back in February. One lady asked for prayer for her stomach. She was told she might have a hernia, and her pain was at a "five." Another lady named Tamisha was on medical leave because she couldn't handle her pains. Her back was in so much pain when she was at work. So, I prayed a general prayer for all of us to be healed from the pains and issues we had been suffering from. After prayer, I asked the lady about her stomach, and she was surprised that the pain was gone, completely at a zero. Hallelujah! We all started to lift our voices in thanks to God! He is so good!

Then I asked Tamisha who had the back issue if she noticed a difference. She said while I was praying, she lifted her hands to receive the prayers and when I spoke to her back to be healed, she felt a popping sensation. Her slipped discs aligned during the prayer. She felt the difference in her neck and back. God left us in amazement. I can't help but think how God aligned me to do this Spirit Lifestyle coaching. I'm happy I took the steps to answer this call. It can be scary to step out in faith to do something you've never done before, but the outcome of obedience is all worth it. I got a feeling that even greater is coming. Glory to Jesus forever. This is the testimony Tamisha sent me.

Testimony

I am so amped up about what is to come from the Holy Spirit. Glory to God. Thank you, coach Elisha, for the word today. Also, for the prayers and healing of my neck and back pain. I'm so honored to be handpicked to go on this spiritual journey. I'm challenging my mind to focus on the Father's business and stay connected with the Spirit. What a beautiful time today.
Tamisha. Michigan.

God is so good, and I really want to do His will. I feel a constant tug to keep going. John 14:11-12 says, "*Just believe that I am in the Father and the Father is in me. Or at least believe because of the work you have seen me do. I tell you the truth, anyone who believes in me will do the same works I have done, and even greater works, because I am going to be with the Father.*"

Seeing the miracles themselves and knowing this has everything to do with the plans of God is the fire behind my drive. I will continue to share all the things that Jesus has done.

PRAYING WITH OUR NEIGHBOR

After coaching a Spirit Lifestyle session, my husband told me that our neighbor was not feeling well. He's a preacher and loves the Lord. He and his beautiful wife serve together in ministry faithfully. He noticed that his walking became a challenge. The doctors tried to find a diagnosis but didn't directly say why these things were happening to him. He went from being totally fine and then suddenly walking and balance became a challenge. His mother had ataxia and eventually was in a wheelchair; others in the family had it as well, so he was thinking it might be a generational thing.

My husband and I took a walk down to his house and found him and his wife sitting in their garage. So, we started talking and just catching up and sharing all that God has been doing. Then he started to tell us about ataxia, that it includes impaired coordination and impaired balance due to damages in circulation, nerves, and muscles. I shared with them that I sensed it was a spiritual attack, that we could stand in agreement and command it to leave in Jesus' name. They agreed to pray. I asked him what his pain level was on a scale from 0-10. He said the pain was a "fifteen." He was sitting in a chair and said even then, it was just constant pain in his legs. I thought to myself, wow, all we can do is give it to God and wait to see what happens.

So, we started to pray and give thanks to God. We then repented, and I encouraged him to forgive anyone who might've hurt him, and to not hold grudges, resentments, disappointments, etc. Church hurt came to mind, and we prayed concerning that as well, that he would let go of it all. He stood up while we were praying and started to sway back and forth. He started to sweat, his breathing became labored, and he began to burp a lot. I sensed this was a manifestation of the spirits that were attacking his body. He was going through deliverance.

Sometimes sickness is tied to a demonic oppression. The more we prayed for any unclean spirits to leave him, the more he burped and even started to try and walk away. We encouraged him to not be afraid. That God was delivering him. I asked him about the pain in his legs, and he said the pain had dropped to a four. The spirits that were tormenting him were leaving. There were several. His wife told us that his ear is clogged also, and that it had been three years since he lost hearing in one of his ears and even had corrective surgery where tubes were put in to drain his ear. So, we continued in prayer for the pain to leave his body, and I put my hand over his ear for it to open in Jesus' name. After a while, his pain was gone, and he said he could hear out of that ear. His wife was crying, and my husband and I were so full of happiness worshiping God. We saw him days later. He said he went fishing and dropped us off a bag of freshly caught fish. He walked some ways up the block and turned and said that he couldn't do that before. He was walking better than before.

For so long, he believed a lie that because people in his family had ataxia and loved God, maybe that's the way it just had to be for him also. We have to trust God with all these things, never coming into agreement with sickness. Believe God for the complete work of salvation, freedom from sin, and sickness. Evil spirits can be driven out because we have the power of God within us. Satan tries to come back and afflict again if there is a door opened. God wants all doors closed from the devil, and only the door of Jesus open. We are not in agreement with the devil. We can't run from or try to tame evil spirits, nor can we cast out the flesh. Evil spirits must be cast out and the flesh under control. With our beloved Holy Spirit, all things are possible.

In the middle of all these wonderful happenings, I received this incredible prophetic word from coach Claire from Spirit Lifestyle. It blew my mind. I give God the glory.

PROPHETIC WORD RECEIVED: DELUGE

"So good to hear from you Elisha! I loved reading what you've been up to with the Holy Spirit. How encouraging! I mentioned on your other post about where Elijah sees the cloud the size of a man's hand when he's praying for rain (1 Kings 18:44), the small beginnings before the deluge.

I believe there is so much more to come as you partner with the Lord! It's not lost on me that your name is Elisha, and Elisha in the Bible inherited a double portion of blessing and anointing following the Prophet Elijah (2 Kings 2:9).

I believe you are entering this season of the double portion. That healing and deliverance are going to be multiplied and come quickly and unexpectedly! You may encounter some people who come against you, but the Lord would encourage you to go where you are welcome and where the people are hungry.

I can see a picture of Cinderella's shoes, and it makes me think that it is your time of favor, of entering your true identity. It makes me think also that you have a pure heart and a compassion for those who are not walking in their true identity, and you're going to help them to know who they are in Christ Jesus and where they fit.

You have a passion for the lost and broken, and have been walking this out faithfully for years. But now the era is changing, and it's a season of restoration and fulfillment of the prayers that have gone before you for many years finally coming into fruition. Of a breaking open of the promises of God, of a rumbling in the earth as the purposes of God are shaken into place, and the enemy is shaken out of his strongholds. Take up your armor and shout a victory shout. You are part of the army of the Lord!"

Claire didn't know this, but one of my childhood nicknames was Cinderella. My siblings used to call me this all the time because of things I used to do around the Berkshire house. This word hit home. My passion is His presence and to help people. I have no other motives than to see others free in Jesus. He is my dream, and my dream has come true. What I've prayed in secret, to serve others, and see breakthrough, it is now happening in the open. It has always happened, but 2020 has been a hard reset. Some people I am no longer connected with, it happened naturally, they used scissors and literally cut the rope on their own. Some people God brought purposely in my life to bless and encourage me, I have no doubt of His divine connections.

Some mindsets I used to have; I no longer have. Everything has changed, and it's because a shifting has happened. It must be the way God intended it to be, what He sees as best. A start of a new way to do what God has been planning and purposing in my heart for years. I knew more was coming, but I could not see what "more" really meant. When I received this word from Claire, I gladly accepted it and said, "Yes, Lord. Let it be so unto me."

I'm blown away at God. Wherever He wants to take me on this adventure, I completely yield. Let us yield to God and not fight His will for us. Trust the author of your life.

SATURDAY, MAY 30, 2020

Today's coaching session was focused on the importance of being filled with the Holy Spirit, but also walking and being led by the Spirit. To do what we can to make sure that we are completely delivered from all contrary spirits, familiar spirits, spirits of religion, spirits of tradition, spirits of pride, things and people we've made into idols, —all things opposite of the Holy Spirit. We must make demons uncomfortable and want to leave. If we make it uncomfortable for evil spirits, it would not be so easy for them to hang around and wreak havoc in our lives. We can get rid of familiar spirits by fasting and praying, seeking after the anointing of the Holy spirit. I shared a process that I use when praying deliverance prayers below. It's self-explanatory.

I encourage people in my sessions to learn it and to use it for self-deliverance or while praying for others. So many have reported deliverance happening in their families and hometowns. This is so awesome. God has given us all authority and power to pray and see change. Just like how we see the evidence of the power working through Elijah and imparted into Elisha (2 Kings 2). Just like we see the evidence of the anointing on Moses (Exodus). It is time for us to step out in faith and not be afraid, think of the Acts of the Apostles. Every principality and power from the enemy (pride, egos, witchcraft, lust, sicknesses etc.) must be expelled.

If you'd like to pray for deliverance over yourself or others, use this mnemonic process (the five "R" words). This is the process used in Chapter 4 as I prayed for Christy from Nigeria who was dealing with a spiritual spouse; revisit that prayer as a reference.

1. **R**ecognize – Acknowledge that help is needed, that there is an evil spirit that must go, and investigate where it stemmed from. Ask the Holy Spirit to reveal things forgotten or hidden.

2. **R**epent – Apologize to God for any opened doors that we've come into agreement with, for any involvement.

3. **R**enounce – Reject any evil spirits through prayer. Reject the agreement. Break the covenant.

4. **R**emove – Separate completely from what was renounced. It can be commanded to leave now that it is renounced, closing the door to the enemy.

5. **R**efill – Replace that space with the Holy Spirit. Invite the Holy Spirit in, filling every compartment, leaving no area untouched. Where the evil used to reside, now the infinite Holy Spirit lives.

If more deliverance is needed after that, start over again with repentance and repeat this process. Do it until there's complete freedom. Contend for it. That's the beauty of prayer. We can do it any time and as many times as required. Then we draw even closer to Jesus and develop an even stronger prayer life. Remember to use this as a guide and allow the Holy Spirit to lead the prayer always.

PRAYER AND ACTIVATION:

God is moving in power, and it is so amazing to me. Why settle for anything less when we can live in the Kingdom realm of God? A life where we are not just using impressive words of human wisdom, but of power and demonstration? I want all that God has for me. If you feel the same, let's talk to the Father together about that:

Dear Heavenly Father,

Thank You for giving all of us access to Your power (Acts 1:8). I want to live where Your manifestations are evident. I don't want to just talk about it; I want to be about it (1 Corinthians 4:20). Forgive me for the moments my faith was not in the right place.

I'm sorry for the times I didn't believe (Mark 9:23-24). My eyes are fixed on You now, and I'm ready for Your rain (Hebrews 12:2). I want my life to be as a well-watered garden (Isaiah 58:11). Demonstrating fruitfulness and productivity always.

I decree and declare that I am connected to Your divine supply system (Philippians 4:19). I cannot be broken, but I remain blessed and fortified (Jeremiah 1:18). My heart is in a place of expectation of Your greatness. You can do all things, and I can do all things through You who lives in me.

I'm endued with power from heaven; therefore, I win, and every spirit that tries to stop what You are doing is paralyzed. I give You center stage of my world to move in power and in might.

I invite You to display Your wonderful deeds and perfections in me and everyone I connect with. Thank You for this blessing. Thank You for a mindset to believe.

In Jesus' name. Amen.

Chapter Six

JUNE MIRACLES

"They begged him to let the sick touch at least the fringe of his robe, and all who touched him were healed."
Matthew 14:36

When I was little, I remembered the safety I felt as I held my dad's hand. I remember the comfort I felt in the hugs from my mother. There's something about the physical touch that makes us feel secure and loved. But no touch has ever compared to being touched by God. Even more so is the privilege to witness how the Lord pours out His Spirit on those who want Him and love Him. Nothing can ever compare to witnessing the Holy Spirit visit our own children and everyone we cross paths with. I've always prayed since my children were born for them to have encounters with Jesus. My husband has always said that our walk should impact our children's lives for the better.

MONDAY, JUNE 1 ,2020

I pray with my children before bedtime, and we pray in the mornings before school. We pray before we eat, and we have Bible discussions often. We use everyday life events as teaching moments. My eight-year-old son is always the first to wake up in the mornings. This morning he woke up with a headache and a terrible crick in his neck. I assumed he was probably laying the wrong way and it resulted in the discomfort he was feeling. He couldn't turn his head to the left nor the right and continued to complain about it. Everyone else was still asleep; it was just he and I. I continued to monitor him as he wore a frown of disapproval on his face. I asked him if he wanted me to pray for him, and he said, "Yes please." Prayer is the norm in our home now, so now I'm focusing on teaching the kids to believe in the power of Jesus for everything.

I put my hand on the back of his neck and prayed. I felt a beautiful warming sensation on my hand but didn't say anything about it. I wanted to see what he was feeling first. I asked him if he was feeling anything. His frown slowly melted away, and his eyebrows raised. I asked him again if he was feeling anything. He said it felt better and followed up with some quick turns of his neck from side to side. He then said he felt warming on his neck while we prayed, that maybe it was the Holy Spirit. I told him that's exactly it, that I felt it also; our beloved Holy Spirit is with us. We just kind of sat there in amazement for a moment and continued to talk about how quickly God moves. His siblings eventually woke up, and he told them what Jesus did with excitement. They will always remember moments like these when they grow older. They will think to pray when in a tight spot. I want to encourage parents to make prayer a norm in the home, to train their children to expect miracles. And document them, it's okay to do that. No matter what in life, we want the children to know that they have help in God, and He's always with them. We have the bible, and we have our journals that are inspired by God.

SATURDAY, JUNE 9, 2020

In our Saturday class this day, we shared about knowing God. How wanting to know Him and His miraculous power can open doors for wonderful things to break out. Expecting miracles and even shining His light in everyday life. Just what if we could touch the hem of His garment with our prayers, praise, and worship?

I once told a coworker about the story in Luke 8:43-44 about the women with the issue of blood that touched the hem of Jesus' garment. I was packing up to go home at the end of a long workday. As I was leaving, I walked back to my desk, and I waved and said hello. My coworker spoke to me and asked how I was doing. I told her I was well, and she started to share how she was not well, but instead worried about an issue she had been facing.

It is not normal for her to share so openly about these issues, but it seems she was worried and desperate. It had already been weeks, and she could not understand why her cycle would not stop. The Holy Spirit brought the story of the lady with the issue of blood to mind (Luke 8:43-48), so I told her about it. She had heard of it before but didn't know it was in the Bible. You could say we had a quick little Bible study at work in that moment.

After going through this passage and making sure she knew where to find this story, I asked her if I could pray for her in the name of Jesus. She's Catholic and said she's not used to that way of praying. But she agreed that I could pray for her in the name of Jesus that this issue would go away. I stated as I prayed for her, just like what was done for the lady we read about, do the same for her Jesus; free her of this issue in Jesus' name.

Weeks went by, and I had not seen her since the day we prayed. But I finally caught up with her and asked her how she was feeling. She didn't know what I was referring to. I had to remind her of our prayer. She then told me that it stopped after we prayed. I was flabbergasted—super excited—but had to contain myself. She was very calm, and I was ready to jump up and down. I reiterated that praying in the name of Jesus is the way to get results. No one can get to the Father except through Him. She agreed. I know that Jesus planted a seed that very day, and she started to read the Bible to get to know His truths. I sent her verses to study and God did the rest. In 1 Corinthians 3:7 it says, "*It's not important who does the planting, or who does the watering. What's important is that God makes the seed grow.*"

I shared this story in our Saturday session, and we all spoke of times when we felt our closest to God. I shared how I've even had prayer closet experiences where I literally felt His presence with me. We all, including the guests, were in the same mindset of partnering with Jesus. Then we prayed and asked God for words of knowledge for one another. I felt led to pray for a foot issue and a business venture. I recorded the sessions and added the links to our community class page. I was later sent a message from a lady named Lisa. She was working and couldn't attend the session live, but just so happened to watch the recording. She said it was for her. She shared a testimony about it, and we were all so encouraged by what she shared. She is now a Spirit Lifestyle coach as well and works strongly in the prophetic. She and her husband have since started a family business called "Hawkins Joyful Bees" where they are beekeepers and have amazing products available for the community, glory to Jesus! Lisa and several others who started out having sessions with me, have felt the calling to start coaching themselves. They share encouraging messages with me about how they are inspired to give it a try. I'm completely amazed, especially since I'm learning myself and would consider myself an average teacher. But that's entirely the purpose of our sessions—to know that we all are used as lights for Jesus. Jesus qualifies us. Every session I have, I encourage people to feel free to start up sessions themselves at their church or with family and friends. Create a scenario where God can show up and shock some folks! God should be seen in every area of our lives—our businesses, neighborhoods, churches, and families. We carry His glory, and when we open our mouths to share of His goodness, good seeds are sown. See Lisa's testimony she shared with the class.

Testimony

I was able to complete the video (of the class recording)...You mentioned feet. I was having issues with my feet, and as you all prayed, I felt the pain completely leave and a tingly sensation. I also felt the glory of God wrapped around my knee all the way to my toes...NO PAIN!! Thank You, Jesus!! You mentioned a business adventure—my husband and I are beginning a business with honeybees. We are beekeepers. What a MIGHTY GOD we serve!
Lisa and Shane. Indiana.

This month has been so full of prophetic words, words of encouragement, and chances to meet new people. That's one of the beauties of stepping out in faith to do ministry. You meet people from all walks of life. And since I've started my Spirit Lifestyle coaching online, it is a bonus to share with people in other countries through technology. We can send an encouraging word to someone that can spark a miracle. I was simply typing a message to a lady who asked for prayer for her family. While praying for her when typing a response, I suddenly heard a high-pitched noise in my ear. I've learned while studying that if I experience something unusual, pray that it is released for whomever

I'm speaking with, or if I am not sure where this symptom came from, I simply pray for God to touch whoever is dealing with it. So, when sending an email, I asked if someone in the home had an ear issue, with ringing noises. She confirmed it, and I encouraged her to pray that it leaves in Jesus' name. This was the testimony sent to me.

TUESDAY, JUNE 23, 2020

Testimony

Jesus revealed to Elisha a problem my husband was having just by her sending me an email. Praise God!

Last night, I did pray over my husband's ears. Before I prayed over my husband, we both started to feel tired. I have never felt tired in the early evening like this. From reading Aliss' books, I realized something is already happening in the spiritual realm. So, we stayed up and decided to pray instead. The first time I prayed over him, it didn't feel like anything happened. Then my husband and I talked and thought maybe it might be an evil spirit, so we looked up the name of the problem online. It was a sickness that developed from hearing loud sounds. We decided to pray again.

I placed my hands on my husband's ears like you said, and I commanded it to go. My husband said while I was praying, he felt something move and something melted in his ear. He also said he felt it come out of his ear. I do have to get used to praying like this. It's very effective. Thank the Lord, Jesus! I am so excited! That's what I want to do; to be used by God always. Hallelujah!

Wow! Isn't that exciting? I love how God uses these moments to spark a new passion within us to want to see more and more of His power at work. Acts 10:38 says, "*And you know that God anointed Jesus of Nazareth with the Holy Spirit and with power. Then Jesus went around doing good and healing all who were oppressed by the devil, for God was with him.*"

This is exactly what God has anointed us to do because of Jesus' sacrifice on the cross. Because we now have access to that same power, we can go and teach and preach and release the healing power of Jesus to anyone who wants to be free, to anyone who wants to experience Him as we do.

Psalms 84:11 says, "*For the Lord God is our sun and our shield. He gives us grace and glory. The Lord will withhold no good thing from those who do what is right.*" I love this passage because it reminds us that if we go and do what God considers good and right, He is going to provide everything that is needed to fulfill His purpose. Stepping out in faith to pray for someone, even when we don't always have the right words, even when we don't know what they might think of us. We must keep in mind, this is good, and this good is worth stepping out and looking crazy for!

The COVID-19 virus numbers at this time continued to spike. So many people were worried, and some were even concerned with the recent lockdowns where food supplies will come from. Now that schools were closed, how will children who depended on eating breakfast and lunch at school, get their meals? I'm thankful in our area there is food distribution at churches like I mentioned in Chapter 4. Now the schools had it also for the community to drive by and load up once a week. My husband and I have continued to pick up pallets full of boxes to distribute. We drove around and looked for people to give boxes of food. We saw an elderly lady who my husband grew up around. She was having back pains, and I asked if I could pray for her when I was dropping the box of food off. She is a Christian believer, so she was happy to accept prayer.

As I prayed for her, the back pain immediately went away. She said, "Wow, that's unbelievable." I told her I thought so too. Jesus is so awesome. We give God all the praise for what He's doing. Then we took off driving to continue to pass out food. That's kind of how it goes. We have to keep moving to save daylight. It's such a blessing to serve Jesus in this way, though. What will He do next? My husband and I just continued our rounds and offering prayers to those who would accept it.

WEDNESDAY JUNE 24, 2020

A friend of our family reached out for prayers concerning his mother. She had been feeling poorly and he connected me with her for a prayer over the phone. She told me that she had arthritis and fibromyalgia. From my experiences and research, fibromyalgia is always an evil demon of pain. She didn't share much with me as we spoke, but I encouraged her to renounce everything that she had come into agreement with that did not line up with her walk with God. She was at a pain level of six (out of ten). She said she felt tingling in her feet as we were praying (she said her feet are normally always hurting), and the pain began to leave. God began to move in her body like she had never seen before. With swollen legs and feet, she could hardly walk around. But twenty-four hours later, I called her up to see how she was feeling, and she said it was an incredibly good day. That she's claiming her healing. The swelling went down on her legs and feet, and she couldn't believe it.

God is still delivering her from some things that she knew about. She went through a lot of traumas in her life, so she's taking it one day at a time. I'm learning that the Holy Spirit reveals what we should renounce when we come to pray for healing. What do we need to let go to reach wholeness again? Pride, anger, holding grudges, unforgiveness—it is not worth our health. I encouraged her to release all that she had been carrying, to follow Jesus fully and without restraint. God is indeed doing it for her. Hallelujah!

This experience made me think of how the disciples renounced everything pertaining to self and took up their cross to follow Jesus. Matthew 16:24 says that Jesus told them if they desired to follow Him, renouncing self was a requirement. To me, that means we are fooling ourselves if we think we can hold on to our selfish thoughts, ways, problems, and traumas, and still follow Jesus effectively. So, there's the option of dying slowly with pains and ailments that come with self. I've noticed that sickness and disease generally stem from unforgiveness (self); Self or the flesh is also the gateway that leads to the burdensome, heavy life of depression. Or there is the option of self-denial. Being willing to endure whatever may come to see the supernatural move of God, and to conform our living to God's way. Simply "If I suffer, I suffer because of my faith in the creator of the universe." I don't know about you, but the choice seems straightforward to me. If we die, we will die giving our all to the one who gave His all for us. Hallelujah!

We must pray for our spiritual eyes to be opened. We can ask the Father to jog the memory of our heavenly life even before we were placed in our mother's womb. Let's ask for glimpses of our time with Him. How He's always been in us, even at times when we didn't know it. He's the beginning and the end, so the trials of this life shouldn't surprise us because it does not surprise Him. By us being inside of Him and Him inside of us, we are one with His divine order. There is no evil so dark nor any demonic entity so powerful that it can stop us because we are all sufficient by His sufficiency. Satan can only control a mind that is open to him. We must close those doors and understand that we are lacking nothing, so we have no need to worry about who did us wrong, hurt us, or disappointed us. We don't have to live in the past and let the devil try to use the bruises as a bookmark to keep us stuck. That's exactly what painful memories will be if we choose not to let it go. A mark, which will continually be revisited and remembered whenever the devil wants to torment us. God is tearing up bookmarks.

He's turned the chapter of our lives and wants us to live out the part where He authorized for us to live whole and free. Just say out loud now, "God, let Your revelation and light flow through my eyes and bring light to my whole body according to Matthew 6:22. I'm ready to live in Jesus' name. I speak with healthy spiritual eyes right now in Jesus' name."

TUESDAY, JUNE 30, 2020

I shared a video on our YouTube channel, a testimony from a lady who was healed from hearing loss. My husband and I were passing out boxes of fresh food again to people in our neighborhood and surrounding cities. It is always such a blessing to meet new people and introduce many to Jesus. Some already know Jesus; some have never heard of Him. We dropped food off at one house and shared Jesus. As we walked away, a little girl asked her daddy who Jesus was. I'm not certain of what good seeds were planted, but I pray she grows up and hears His name several times and never forget this day when they learned how much Jesus loves them. This is why we were going door to door.

We had opportunities to pray for some people again. We stopped by a housing complex where several families were outside, and one guy was fixing on his car. As we passed out food and offered prayers, the man fixing the car asked if we could drop a box of food to a lady who lives in a senior citizen's home. We would have to drive just a few miles away. We told him "Absolutely, we'd be glad to." Once we wrapped up things at the housing complex, he sent a message to the lady informing her that we were coming, and we took the drive to the address he gave us.

Once we arrived, we had challenges getting in. The buzzer didn't seem to work and when we called up, she wasn't answering. We had to try a few more times before the door was unlocked for us. Once we found her floor, we figured out why it was hard to get in. She couldn't hear us, she hardly heard the buzzer to let us in. We had on our masks, and

I tried to talk with her, but she could not hear a word I was saying, so I pulled my mask down briefly, standing away down the hall, and told her of the man who asked us to drop off food to her. She read my lips and invited us to drop off the food.

Once we established the right room she was in, my husband went back down to the car to grab all the things we were going to give her. She was talking loudly because her ears were clogged and was thanking us for stopping by. I thought to myself, "This dear lady lives here by herself. God doesn't want her ears clogged. What if I offered to pray and God opens her ears?" God did it for our neighbor last month! Surely, He could do it again.

I gestured to her ears and then held my hands together in a praying motion, back and forth. I was hoping she would understand that I was asking if I could pray. She said "Sure," and then closed her eyes and lifted her hands in surrender. I said, "Wow, okay, that was easy!" I stepped closer to her and hovered my hands over her ears and said, "I command the spirit of deafness to leave now in the name of Jesus." Then I said, "Holy Spirit, free her ears. She needs help. You love her so much! This deafness is not from you. I speak clear ears now in Jesus's name."

That's about it. I stepped back and snapped my fingers at each ear and her eyes blinked tightly and then opened and then widened with excitement. I asked her, "Can you hear me?"

She screamed, "Yes, I can hear you!"

Then she launched forward and gave me the biggest hug I've ever had. She was so appreciative. She was rejoicing in Jesus! I was happy also, but I just stood there in awe. God just opened her ears, whoa! My husband came up with the rest of the boxes. When he walked in, she was talking to him and he was responding, then she responded back to him. He didn't notice right away that she could hear him, although we all had our masks on. So, I got his attention. I told him to notice that she can hear him and respond without issues like before.

He stopped in his tracks and said, "Wow what happened? Did you guys pray?"

The lady said, "Yes, she prayed for me, and Jesus cleansed my ears."

Jesus is so amazing. I asked if I could record her testimony in that very moment. She gladly shared in the video the statement below. I'm so thankful for all that God did for this sweet lady. We give Him all the glory.

Testimony

She prayed, and the Lord heard her, and He cleansed my ears. I can hear! I thank God and I thank her.

When asked how long her ears were shut, she added,

It's been going on for a couple of years, I had hear-

ing aids and they broke. I thank Jesus. Hallelujah.
Bernice. Michigan.

It is moments like these that make me fall more and more in love with sharing about Jesus. God has shown me time and time again. We don't have to be famous; we don't need great lights and music. We don't need to be in a special place to be used by God. He wants to touch ordinary and everyday people by using ordinary and everyday people like you and me. The only way we will see the actions of God is if we act on what He told us to do. Like the acts of the Apostles.

Smith Wigglesworth said, "The Acts of the Apostles was written because the apostles acted!"

What would happen if all of us acted on faith and went out into all the world and preached, and shared testimonies with not just our local church, but people all around? People we've never met before.

Matthew 9:37-38 says, "*The harvest is plentiful, but the workers are few. Ask the Lord of the harvest, therefore, to send out workers into his harvest field.*" I feel revival is happening right now, and God is calling us all to go. It is happening in us individually and in our homes first. Jesus did not ask us if we wanted to go. Just like He told the disciples in Mark 16:15, He simply said, "Go!" That's the first word of that verse. "*Go into all the world and preach the Good News to everyone.*" I heard someone say that if we don't go, it is like going to work and telling our boss to do our job for us. We would never do that! We go to work and fulfill our duties. Sometimes going is just the ministry of presence to encourage someone through a tough time. We might not see the complete fulfillment of what God is doing, but it is not our job to change situations. It's just our job to go in faith, speaking in faith activates miracles.

God is the one who does the converting, the saving, the convicting, the convincing, the healing. Although we have the power to pray and see healings, miracles, and deliverances, we have to remember to stay open to how God wants to move. We have one job: step out in faith, then let God move and have His way. If we don't go, God will raise up someone else who is thirsty, humble, and willing to yield everything to work for the Kingdom of God. Hallelujah!

This is what the acts of the Apostles were all about. They stepped out and acted on the Word and what Jesus taught them. We acted on faith as we continued to pass out food. We delivered at another lady's house. After passing out food, I asked if she had any prayer requests. She told us that she had cancer several times and recovered. She went through the chemo processes and everything. There was a tumor that appeared under her left breast, and she wanted us to stand in agreement with her that it would not be cancerous and that she would not have to go through that chemo again. She had a follow-up doctor's appointment in a few days, and they were going to do the necessary testing to see what's going on.

I asked her to place her hand on the location of the lump, and I placed my hand on her shoulder. I commanded in the name of Jesus for the lump to leave her body. I know she asked me to pray for it to not be cancer, but I figured why not command it to leave her body all together in Jesus' name? That the root of it would be destroyed and that she would get a clean bill of health from the doctors. We told her we would see her the next week when it was time to pass out food again. She said that she will have an update by then and will let us know how it goes.

The following week came, and we did our rounds again. When my husband walked up to her door to drop the food off, she sprung from her screen door with excitement. She said before going to the doctor's appointment, she read Psalms 30:1-3, "*I will exalt you, Lord, for you rescued me. You refused to let my enemies' triumph over me. O Lord my God, I cried to you for help, and you restored my health. You brought me up from the grave, O Lord. You kept me from falling into the pit of death.*" Hallelujah!

She told us the doctors could not find the tumor. She was given a clean bill of health. Glory to Jesus forever! God's Word is true, the Kingdom of heaven is now, and the Kingdom of heaven is the person of Jesus Christ who lives in us. Having faith in that makes us whole. Miracles are activated by someone who believes.

PRAYER AND ACTIVATION:

It is impossible to go on as usual once we've been touched by God. We are taken into a brand-new way of thinking. Our eyes are open to encompass how life is really meant to be. The more we go after Him will create more possibilities of unprecedented joy and increase in every area of life. If this is your desire, let's talk to the Father about it together:

Dear Heavenly Father,

Thank You that everyone can have direct access to You. Although some have never known the love of an earthly father, You are always there. I want to draw so close to You, I want to touch You daily, and I want my life to be positioned in the right course that will cause me to experience divine intimacy. I submit to meditating and studying everything about You so that I can be nurtured (Psalms 1:2), developed, and fortified, to have a victorious life that You've purposed for me. Thank You that my spirit is enabled from every side. That no matter what's going on in the world, my focus shall remain to dwell in Your secret place, I am safe under Your shadow (Psalms 91). Thank You for wisdom to champion over the wrong mentality (Joshua 1:7-8). To reject Satan, and his lies that would cause me to doubt Your nearness (James 4:7). I will not fall for it, convincing me that I'm alone, that I'm limited. No way! I'm in partnership and fellowship with You, my dear Father, with precious Jesus, and my beloved Holy Spirit (2 Corinthians 13:14). Angels are dispatched for my favor, and as I draw closer and closer to You, I'm made a distributor of Your eternal works in my world. The power, dominion, and authority of darkness has no effect on me.

I'm in the world but not of it. I live in the presence of the Almighty God. I draw close to touch You. You touch me and my life is changed forever. I'm in my rightful place and I say out loud & declare that "God has ordained and approved of me." I have joy, faith, increase, and true love. In Jesus' name. Amen.

Chapter Seven

JULY MIRACLES

"Look, I have given you authority over all the power of the enemy, and you can walk among snakes and scorpions and crush them. Nothing will injure you." Luke 10:19

It has been an amazing journey, a humbling one. I wake each day wondering what God will do next, looking in great expectation. One thing is for sure: it is by His power that we are all saved. It is by His might that we have authority to overcome the oppressor. God created us in His image and likeness, not to try to be like gods, but understanding that He is our Father and there's an inheritance that comes with that. We can operate in authority as a commander of the heavenly army. We can speak into the atmosphere and create. We can decree and declare healing for souls. The requirement is that we live righteously so that we can rule in this world. We are not the enemy's door mat; he is the doormat. Our citizenship is in heaven and this world has nothing on the power that we have access to as the children of God. We are called to create, carry, and release the glory of God everywhere we go.

THURSDAY, JULY 2, 2020

I look for opportunities to release the healing power of Jesus and had that opportunity again when I visited my dad's church. The lockdown has really changed how the local churches would have worship services. It's all virtual. My husband and I met up with my dad, Pastor Upshaw, and offered to train staff to do a full virtual production and how to stream it. We met and had discussions on recordings, lights, cameras, editing, music, all of it, and it turned out so well. Glory to Jesus!

We had a lot of fun working, and we know it is always an honor to serve leadership, better still our earthly father, to offer tools from our company to push his vision and to keep the message of Jesus going despite the enemy trying to stop it during this pandemic. We were wrapping up to leave after a session. Before walking out, my dad told me that he had a cyst on his left shoulder. It was like the size of half an egg. He told me that right before the pandemic hit, he noticed it. He scheduled a doctor's appointment earlier in the year, but it was postponed because of COVID-19. Every week, the cyst was getting bigger and bigger, and they kept pushing the appointment further and further out.

I put my hand on my dad's shoulder and thanked God for him and that He wanted my dad to be healed. I commanded the cyst to leave his body in Jesus' name. Nothing seemed to happen, but we still praised God and sealed our agreement. We left the church giving thanksgiving. Like when Jesus healed the lepers, Luke 17:14 says, "*And as they went, they were cleansed.*" The next day, my dad told me that the cyst went down; he noticed a big difference. Hallelujah! We prayed and thanked God for what was happening. That God would complete the work. I know that God does all things well. That He does nothing partially. By the third day, my dad said the cyst was just about gone. Glory to God! Here's his testimony:

Testimony

I went to the doctors in March, and he gave me a script to call St. John hospital for an ultrasound that they scheduled in April. Before I could go, it was canceled because of COVID-19. They have not rescheduled yet. Since then, the cyst on my shoulder has been getting a little bigger every week. I asked Elisha to pray for me when we were doing broadcasting work. After prayer...three days later, it is just about gone. I'm feeling it now, and it is smaller than yesterday! My Lord!

(Update: Noticed weeks later that the cyst was completely gone.)

Pastor Lorris Upshaw Jr. Michigan.

(L-R: Grandkids Elisha, Dameon Jr. and Salah)

SATURDAY, JULY 11, 2020

I'm so excited about Saturday sessions. I just know that God is up to something. I'm always surprised along with everyone else. We never know how He will move, but we are so loving it and ready for all that God wants to do. Hallelujah!

Different people are coming through to our sessions weekly. One was a pastor named Ben Odongo from Uganda. He would pray for healings and miracles often but stopped as a heavy spirit came with the pandemic. This COVID-19 lockdown has started to take its toll on many. This has been a common attack from the enemy. A spirit of heaviness, oppression, depression, and grief has swept through the land. We renounce these spirits in our sessions and command it to leave. We choose to close the door and yield our focus and hearts to Jesus, inviting the Holy Spirit to come and remove all things that should not be.

This is a spiritual war which we know is good versus evil. When we commit to God and turn away from the world, it can be compared to us all walking in sync or facing the same way. Then suddenly the believer turns their life around, no longer walking in sync with the world. Now the believer is facing the opposite of the world. Imagine walking through a crowd. Trying to move forward when so much is against you, that would be a challenge. But it is written in 1 John 5:4-5, "*...For everyone born of God is victorious and overcomes the world; and this is the victory that has conquered and overcome the world—our [continuing, persistent] faith [in Jesus the Son of God].*" This is the successful formula of the believer. This is what Pastor Ben recognized.

Here is the feedback Pastor Ben sent, he has given me permission to share it.

Testimony

Hello Elisha Brown, thanks for the great ministry you do. You guys blessed my heart. I got to know about the Zoom meeting through my fiancée. Thanks to her for linking me up with you. After yesterday's class fellowship on Zoom, I continued intimately with deep meditations with the Holy Spirit. Usually, I wake up early to pray. After my prayer time as usual, I went to bed to sleep, and when I woke, I was speaking in tongues seriously. After that, I started worshiping in a song and later on, I found myself singing a totally new song with a new rhythmic flow and tune. The words of the songs were in the tongues of the Holy Spirit, and I was singing it like a normal song and after that song, the same continued for about two more new songs. And I continued in prayer.

With the heaviness of the lockdown, I kind of relaxed on healing ministry and many people have been wanting me to pray for them, including a lady in India, but I was always giving excuses and I end up not doing it. Now yesterday in the Zoom meeting, I got so activated, and I felt the life and the zeal that had gone down in me had come back. Trust me, I started seeing myself walking in the miracle ministry again. The "Spirit Lifestyle" video you showed us on Zoom helped me a lot.

Tears came down my eyes and I told the Holy Spirit I will never give excuses again. This made me pick up the phone and call the lady in India who had been a patient and was bedridden for quite a while at home, and this morning, she was still on drip, so the family had started losing hope. I spoke the word of healing through a phone call, and she instantly got healed. She even got up from the bed by herself and tried to remove the drip from her hands until the home nurse came and advised her to wait, and she helped her take it off.

She says she is now feeling fine. For sure the power that works in a believer is real. I even shared the testimony to encourage my father. So, in my WhatsApp status and in some WhatsApp groups, I told people who are seriously sick or have someone who is bedridden to inbox me privately. Since morning, I have been just doing healing ministry via phone calls with different people. I have just got out of my room at least to get something to eat. The Zoom session is what did the serious activation of what had gone dormant in me, and now I am so consumed by the zeal. Thanks so much. I am so excited with the fire in me. I just feel I am another man.

~ *Pastor Ben and Agnes.* Uganda.

TUESDAY, JULY 14, 2020

I received a prayer request from a dear lady that has known me all my life. As far back as I can remember, she's always been devoted to God. She wanted to tell me what was going on with her, and after seeing the testimonies I've shared on social media, she was encouraged that God would heal her also. So, I called her over to pray over the phone. She told me that spiritual warfare was going on with her, that she was suffering from pains in her body. I asked her if she could rate her level of pain on a scale of 1-10. She said it was at a nine, and she was told that she had severely inflamed muscles. She was prescribed medicines, but nothing was working.

Just like Pastor Ben, she's a believer who is facing planned opposition from the enemy. The enemy wants us to doubt that we can be free, that we are victorious, that we can live a life whole through Jesus. And for those who are devoted to ministry, Satan wants to discourage them and tire them out so they'll give up on contending. She had a choice to make: focus on the pains in her body, trusting in the diagnoses that were given to her, or to keep contending for her healing. She chose the latter. Hallelujah!

Mark 11:23 says, "*For verily I say unto you, that whosoever shall say unto this mountain, be thou removed, and be thou cast into the sea; and shall not doubt in his heart but shall believe that those things which he saith shall come to pass; he shall have whatsoever he saith.*" We joined in prayer and like this scripture says, chose not to doubt in our hearts.

Of course, the enemy will bring fear and worry to our minds. But that's when we make a choice to cast away those thoughts and listen to God's heart. This is so powerful to be heart-to-heart with God. Hiding His words in our heart. Believing with our heart like this sister did. She had a beautiful encounter during our prayer and God took away her pain completely. From a nine to a zero. Here is her testimony she shared with me.

Testimony

Praise God the Lord Jesus has triumphed over my enemy. My testimony begins thirteen weeks ago during the COVID-19. The Lord had given me to start an Intercessors prayer group with the Intercessors at my church. I would call them, and we would pray for two hours. About the second week in, I started to have a pain on the left side of my body. We prayed about it, and I received a release from the pain for a couple of days. My church prayed, I received release for days. But it would come back. This battle went on for twelve weeks. I went to my doctor during the ninth week. They gave me pain meds and muscle relaxers, but nothing worked. Had an X-ray done, but no broken bones. Conclusion was severely inflamed muscle. The week of July 6, I just so happened (lead to by the Holy Ghost) to pick up my phone. I was looking through Facebook (I had not been on Facebook for a while) and saw a testimony from sister Elisha about someone receiving healing after they prayed. Now, I am not new to healing after prayer. Throughout my Christian walk, I have been healed. I called Elisha. I explained to her what was going on. And

as she began to talk, the Holy Ghost filled my living room. And as she prayed the pain went away, completely. I got up and started doing things I could not do. I walked into my bedroom and the presence of God was there too. I am walking in my healing. Oh, the enemy tried, but I said not so. Jesus healed me, and that's my testimony. God will always use a yielded, available vessel that is submitted to Him. Thank you, sister Elisha Brown. May the Lord Jesus continue to bless you. Love my sister. Felicia with (daughter) KiLisa. Michigan.

WEDNESDAY, JULY 15, 2020

God blessed us to link up with a church in India. The pastor shares the same name as me. He said I stood out to him, and he knew that it was God leading him to connect with my husband and I. We've been chatting and sharing about Jesus. We had prayer calls and even scheduled a Zoom conference for his church where my husband and I shared the exciting things happening. Grace Church in India loves God, and they had several who were seeking to be free from some things, to be healed and delivered. It is so interesting how years ago, I could not even imagine praying for healing for people in another country over Zoom. But now we all know God is showing up, and that there is no distance in His Spirit. That He created time and distance, but He's not subject to it, just like He created the heavens and the earth, but He is not limited to borders or nationalities. In person or over Zoom, we were all expecting a mighty move of God.

When we have faith and truly believe God like this, awesome, supernatural things can happen without limits. That makes me think of the centurion in Matthew 8. The centurion approached Jesus asking for a miracle. His servant was sick at home, paralyzed and suffering terribly. Jesus offered to go and heal the boy, but the centurion interjected in verse 8-9, saying, "*But the officer said, 'Lord, I am not worthy to have you come into my home. Just say the word from where you are, and my servant will be healed. I know this because I am under the authority of my superior officers, and I have authority over my soldiers. I only need to say, "Go," and they go, or "Come," and they come. And if I say to my slaves, "Do this, they do it.*" Jesus was really amazed at this. People during that time only displayed faith in Jesus if He went with them, touched Him, or Jesus physically touched them. Someone with this kind of faith was remarkable.

He was a Roman officer, which means he wasn't an Israelite. The Roman officers were hated by the Jews because of how the Romans mistreated them. God is raising up people from all walks of life—some who have never known Jesus, some newly introduced to Him, some who will see more miracles, signs, and wonders than those who've called themselves devout Christians. This world, its religion, and its traditions have caused darkness, separation, and delusions to enter into the hearts of many. But God has a remnant near and far who is hungry and knows revival is happening. It is going to require faith.

This Roman officer could have allowed so many things to get in the way of his belief. Fear of the unknown, pride because he knew he was hated, money, language, race, distance, and time. But He chose to believe Jesus without barriers or blockages. Jesus wants us to have faith like this. Jesus turned to him in verse 13 and said, "*Go home. All that you have believed for will be done for you*!" And his servant was healed at that very moment. There is no distance in the Spirit; there are no limits to what God can do. The power of Jesus is for everyone. I had this in mind as I had this Zoom conference with "Grace Ministries" in India.

My husband and I shared about Jesus and learned to pause in between each thought and statement so that Pastor Elisha could translate. I didn't know what to expect. I've never done this before, needing a translator. It was a unique experience. After we taught, we instructed them to put their hands on any ailments, and we prayed and invited the Holy Spirit to come. Completely yielding to Him moving over us. We released the power of Jesus by faith. Repenting of every sin or agreement made, closing any doors that were opened to familiar spirits, ancestral spirits, idol worship and fears. We told sicknesses, pains, and fevers to leave. Many were touched and blessed by the conference. Many breakthroughs occurred because of the faith of the people there, many. Hallelujah!!

~Pastor Elisha (Grace Ministries Zoom Conference) – Vijayawada, India

TUESDAY, JULY 21, 2020

The internet has us connected all over the world. The enemy uses it for sure to push his agenda, but it can be used to push the Kingdom of God also. That's if we choose to use our platforms for Jesus. All my social media pages are devoted to Jesus and my experiences of living a Holy Spirit lifestyle in every area. I want Jesus to be pleased with my life online and offline. I think that's what the pages are for; it is another tool to use to show the light of Jesus. I told God He can have it for His use. That's how He connected me to Pastor Elisha.

I didn't like the internet at first because I saw how the enemy used it to push all sorts of sin, vanity, pride, backbiting, sexual sins, and seducing people into going after the world's standard of success. I saw how the enemy wants so badly to be in every place at once, but he's not God; he's not omnipresent, so the world wide web is the only way he can travel and promote his devilish works. God is omnipresent and already has all things planned out, so He is literally showing ministries all over the world how to use the web to spread the gospel. I've prayed for so many people that I've never met. I'm seeing the deluge in real time. Many souls are still lost, and many are not completely free from torment. We have to keep working, releasing what Jesus has freely given to us to others.

My husband was online and saw a classmate from years ago. Sometimes when online, God may highlight someone to you. When my husband saw her picture, a word of knowledge came to his mind for her. She's from Texas, and the last time he saw her, they were teens. God, however, had been with her every year of her life and saw her situation and aligned us to share with her. He set up a time to call her. Once we were speaking with her, she shared that she suffered a lot over the years with migraines; every year the pain continued to get worse until it was running her life. The day we spoke to her, she said her pain level was a twenty on a scale from 0-10. Ouch! The enemy was really having a field day on her. She didn't understand why this was happening to her.

My husband shared what God revealed to him. That it had everything to do with forgiveness. She went through a traumatic life event fifteen years ago, and Satan used the hurt and disappointment from it to sneak in and cause affliction on her body. It was inward hurt and devastation that went undetected and continually grew until there were outward manifestations of pain in the body. Literally the moment she went through a traumatic divorce, that's the same time her migraines started. Once she was aware of how she was being fought, she made a conscious decision to renounce the pains, the hurts, forgiving who was involved and just surrendering it all by laying everything and everyone at the feet of Jesus. At that moment, every painful memory, every spoken word, every deed done to hurt her, she no longer had on her shoulders. She repented for holding all of it for fifteen years in her heart. She wanted to forgive fully so that the Father in heaven would forgive her.

Matthew 6:14 says, "*For if you forgive others their trespasses [their reckless and willful sins], your heavenly Father will also forgive you.*" The tears were falling like a gentle waterfall as I watched her countenance change. It was as though we could see the glow of Jesus pour over her like love and wrap around her like a garment. The heaviness and pain melted away like Psalms 97:5, "*Mountains melt away like wax in a fire when the Lord of all the earth draws near.*" That's exactly what happened for her.

After prayer, we asked her to check for the pain. She said she didn't feel anything. This was the first time in fifteen years she didn't feel anything; the pain was gone. Hallelujah! That's our Jesus! My eyes began to swell up with tears at the thought of God's love for us. He never intended for us to hurt. That's all the enemy's doing. He uses sin sick, hurting people to hurt other people. But when we have Him, we have all we need. Here is the testimony shared with me:

Testimony

I have been having migraines for the past fifteen years or so. No amount of medicine I took helped. My doctors couldn't figure out why I kept getting them, and they seemed to get worse and worse every year. They have been so bad to the point I can't sleep, blurred vision, nausea, you name it. They have caused me to have so much tension in my neck and back at times. Only thing that would truly kind of help is to just lay down in the dark. Dameon told me he needed to talk with me about these migraines because he knew I had been having them for way too long. I called him and he had me read a Scripture that the Holy Ghost brought on his spirit to talk with me about forgiveness. Once I forgave whom I needed to forgive, those migraines would go away. I tell you between him and sister Elisha praying with me, Lord I can't

even explain the release I felt after. I went from the migraine being a "twenty" on a scale of 1-10 to a true zero. No headache at all, no tension. Jesus works in mysterious ways through some wonderful people. That is my testimony I would like to share. Thank you so much sister Elisha and brother Dameon Brown for being inserted into my life at the right time. Continue to be the blessings that Jesus have you here to be. Much love and respect to you all!
Shalise. Texas.

FRIDAY, JULY 30, 2020

It sure has been different working from home. I'd never done this before on a month-to-month basis. My engineering project that would normally require me to be in the lab was just postponed. Everyone was working from home due to the pandemic. Now my days are full of reviewing electrical schematics, organization meetings, and engineering training. I did, however, receive a call on this day to go into the lab to support a technician who was working on another project, to discuss wiring and possible schematic changes. I arrived to find out that there was some sort of confusion or mix-up; there was no problem as the technician had originally thought. So, about an hour after I arrived, I was heading back home.

I just so happened to see an engineer that I hadn't seen in a long time. I was surprised to see him there. Even before the pandemic, he was out on medical leave for quite some time. We got to chatting and he mentioned that he was heading to another doctor for an annual checkup of a tumor that's next to his pancreas. The doctors have been keeping watch to make sure it does not turn into cancer. Normally when someone mentions having to see the doctor, an issue they have, or pain they're in, I take it as a personal invitation to ask if I can pray for them. I asked him had he prayed or had someone else prayed for him yet for the tumor to leave. He smiled and said "No," then I asked if I could be the first one to pray for him. He said, "You want to pray for me right now?"

I said, "Yes, I want to." He told me to go ahead, so I did. I asked him to put his hand where the tumor was. Without touching, I shadowed where his hand was and commanded that tumor to leave his body in the name of Jesus! Releasing the power of Jesus so that it would disappear. Never to come back. All this in the middle of the lab with a few other on looking engineers. They kind of know me by now. I'll pray in a hot second!

It is written in 1 Thessalonians 5:17, "*Never stop praying.*" Not just the prayers on our knees, but to always have an attitude of prayer. Whether home in the prayer closet or at work in the middle of a lab discussing wiring. The attitude of continual prayer is built on acknowledging that God is always with us, and we totally need Him for everything. To have a consciousness of Christ, His omnipresence, and yielding to Him in obedience. This kind of relationship with God causes authentic and spontaneous prayers like the short prayer I prayed for the technician.

I couldn't keep him there standing all day. I didn't want to make him uncomfortable; we can't assume everyone prays the same way. I'm not ashamed, but we don't always know the hearts of those we are praying for, so we need to remember to be considerate when they give us the honor of praying for them. Short prayers are few in words but very mighty in power. Hallelujah! We can do the long prayers in our private prayer times; we should do it as often as we can. The short prayers are more effective and show the growth of the long prayers. We just get stronger and stronger.

The technician thanked me for the short prayer and said when he finally goes to get that checkup, he'll let me know what the doctor says. He's retiring soon, and with the way the pandemic and lockdown was going, I was not sure I'd see him again before his last day. But he said if the tumor is gone, that would flip his mind about everything. I was rejoicing on the inside because that statement from him made me realize that he was a skeptic. A brilliant technician, in his sixties, but hadn't had an encounter with Jesus yet. Could this be his Jesus encounter? Could it be God orchestrated for me to come into the lab today? For him to randomly tell me about a tumor? For me to offer him a short prayer? For Jesus to open his eyes to the truth of His existence and that He loves him so much?

Wow. That's just like our Jesus. Some prayers are answered immediately. Sometimes we have to wait to see what God does. It is all about God's timing. If I never see this technician again, I'm super happy that we had this prayer together in the lab. Gods got plans for him. I pray he has more and more encounters with Jesus.

PRAYER AND ACTIVATION:

Can we believe that God gives us the power and authority to alter situations and circumstances? It can sound too good to be true, but it's our reality as His children. We are His offspring, and the Word is our guide. I truly believe this. Let's confess it. Let's talk to the Father together.

Dear Heavenly Father,

Thank You for adopting us all into Your family. We are royalty, and the adversary knows it (Ephesians 1:5). Satan must be so jealous of us and our relationship with You, hence the attacks he tries to send.
I believe that I am Your offspring and that my life is meant to experience Your supernatural realities (Acts 17:29). That Your immortal and incorruptible life through Christ is at work in me.
My mindset is above sicknesses, darkness, and all effects of the carnal human nature. Thank You for giving me the authority to stand strong and decree Your Word over me and others I stand in faith with (Matthew 28:18). I am an associate of the God-kind, manifesting your glory and divinity. You created me to have a life full of peace, divine health, and godly grace. Transform me, Father, until what I see in a mirror is Your image. Teach me all things and strengthen me for this journey.
Help me when my disbelief tries to surface. Never let me forget the authority You've afforded me to trample on every snake and scorpion (Luke 10:19).
Never let me forget that I am one with You spirit to spirit, heart to heart, and mind to mind. My life is full of beauty and excellence because of

Jesus.

I believe this, and miracles will be activated because of my belief.

In Jesus' name. Amen.

Chapter Eight

AUGUST MIRACLES

"But you will receive power when the Holy Spirit comes upon you. And you will be my witnesses, telling people about me everywhere—in Jerusalem, throughout Judea, in Samaria, and to the ends of the earth." Acts 1:8

FRIDAY, AUGUST 7, 2020

It is auditioning time again. Another model after Christ's opportunity. I received a call for a commercial opportunity for a dog treats company. These are always a pleasant change of pace for me. I powder my nose and dress the part and prepare to improv. The little dogs on set were the cutest. Reminded me of my childhood dog named Sheba. She was like a sister to us kids. I'm assuming that could be the reason I agreed to the audition.

But the more I thought of it, I prayed asking the Holy Spirit to prepare me in case this is another modeling missions' opportunity, a time to share about Jesus. Every modeling experience I've had, someone was strategically placed there for me to share about Jesus. When I arrived, we followed all the safety COVID protocols as they matched us up as on-screen families. Each play family had a mom, dad, and daughter. The scenes took place at a park, and we were to pretend to be having a family picnic and sitting together with the dog.

They placed me as a mother and introduced me to my pretend husband. Then in walked the little girl that would be our on-screen daughter. Her biological mother followed behind her wearing a surgical boot. I felt God was highlighting her to me. I wondered if she was the reason God sent me to this audition. As we waited to be called in for the audition, I again asked the Holy Spirit to guide me, to give me an opportunity to speak with her if I am to pray for her.

We went through the audition and were done in a matter of minutes. We were released and started walking out. We were heading in the same direction. We started talking about the audition experience and whether we felt we nailed it! I noticed that we parked directly next to each other.

I ended up asking her about her foot and the boot she was wearing. She said it was fractured, a torn ligament, and she was hoping it heals properly and that she would not require surgery. She also said that they drove three hours one way so that her daughter could audition.

I asked her if I could pray for her safe travels back and that she would not need surgery. I told her I was a Christian minister and don't believe in coincidences. That I noticed her foot the moment she walked through the door and that I would love to pray for her.

She was nice and allowed me to pray. I spoke a word of encouragement to her telling her that Jesus loves her very much and that He does not want her to be in pain. I spoke to the ligament, tendons, muscles, bones, the fracture, and commanded it to be healed and mended in the name of Jesus. For the healing power of Jesus to completely cover her. That the Holy Spirit would flow through her from her head to her feet. I prayed that as she drove back that they would be safe and that she would experience the peace, love, and presence of God. She wiggled her boot a bit and said "Wow, thank you," and was hopping in the car as her daughter looked on. I quickly told her I wish her the absolute best in everything, then she was gone.

I thought to myself as I was heading back home, a few scenarios. What if the girl and I are booked for the job officially and will have to work together again in a few weeks? Her mother may have a wonderful story to tell of what became of her foot. Or what if there were no bookings and my assignment was to just be there to pray for her after that long drive. That it was a divine encounter for her to hear about Jesus. Either way I know the Holy Spirit is working for her, and I'm so happy to have been there to let her know that He put her on my mind, that He's always thinking about her.

SATURDAY, AUGUST 8, 2020

I had wanted to have weekly Spirit Lifestyle sessions in person by this point, but due to the pandemic, it seems Zoom is a tool that I'll be using for a while. We shared on the topic of healings on this day. I encouraged all the participants to invite friends who need prayer and who are looking for healing through Jesus. To testify of what Jesus has been up to. We had a few people come for the first time, and God moved again in power. I'm learning the power of sharing the testimony of Jesus.

We shared testimonies of all the miracles that are taking place around us and to us personally. We could feel the atmosphere in our homes starting to shift. The grace for miracles to happen again. Evil spirits can't stand the presence of Jesus. When He's invited in, things must change. It is His love for us that's so strong, and every spiritual darkness must leave because of that love. It is not how loud we scream, commanding evil spirits to go; it is not by pushing someone down on the floor by laying hands; it is not by how loud the musicians play; it is not by our might; it is not by our power. It's by the Spirit of the Lord.

A lady requested prayer for the tumors in her liver and pancreas to dissolve. She said she had chills all over at random times, and on top of all that. As we stood in agreement to pray with her. She said she felt the presence of the Holy Spirit. We prayed for physical and mental healing, that she would receive the complete overall restoration from Jesus. She noticed her chills went away, and she was starting to feel at peace! Hallelujah! She will be going to the doctors soon to check up on the tumors.

Another lady named Sharon joined from Florida who felt there was a curse on her life. She was always feeling a weight in her stomach, an elephant in her stomach she called it, and sometimes something crawling up her back, which is very strange. She had headaches with pains in her upper back and neck. She said her pain was at a five out of ten during the session. As I prayed for her, she felt the weight in her stomach slowly going away and the headache and back and neck pain completely left. We prayed and commanded the curse to be broken from that moment in Jesus' name. She is free and sent me the following testimony:

Testimony

This was my first time joining the Saturday season (8/8/20) (New Beginning). I had been suffering with a headache, back neck pain, and felt like an elephant was sitting on my stomach for over five months. I was miserable! I asked for prayer. Before the end of the prayer, my headache was completely gone. The "elephant" on my stomach started releasing, and my pain left. Hallelujah! I praise God for healing me! I thank God for Elisha and those on the Zoom call for praying for me and standing in agreement with me! God is a healer and deliverer!

~*Sharon.* Florida.

SATURDAY, AUGUST 11, 2020

I dreamt of the harvesting of souls last night. It was interesting what I saw, but I will try to explain. I saw myself pregnant, carrying twins. I felt the spiritual meaning of that was that double was coming. When I woke from the dream, I remembered what I felt and how I took care, and the preparations that I took in expectancy of what was to come. I was aware of the womb and how the babies were mixed with different nationalities. I felt this meant that God is birthing purpose within us as believers. That as we yield to Him and follow His plans, we will cross denominations, cultures, traditions, countries, and ethnic groups. It reminds me of Matthew 9:36-38: "*When he saw the crowds, he had compassion on them because they were confused and helpless, like sheep without a shepherd. He said to his disciples, The harvest is great, but the workers are few. So, pray to the Lord who is in charge of the harvest; ask him to send more workers into his fields.*"

Wherever God sends us, if we go, He will use us to impact our world. He will take us into different dimensions, different ways of thinking, using different strategies and methods to win souls for Jesus. I never thought I would have reached as many countries as I have, ministering to hungry hearts and praying for healing and deliverances. All while the border is closed to most countries.

God is not limited to a border. Closing the border did not stop Him from moving, healing, and delivering. Just like He is not limited to one-on-one prayers. Right over the internet, He heals. Some were sick and while reading a testimony of someone else's healing, they in turn were healed. As I shared testimonies, the faith and expectancy of others grew, some were healed just by listening. Hallelujah!

The possibilities are endless. This is the one true God we are talking about. Like Elisha asked Elijah for a double portion, everything is doubled for the believers right now if they yield to God: the impact, the anointing, and the blessings. Glory to God!!

My stomach was huge in this dream, and I was intentional about taking great care to not hurt what I was carrying. It would be horrible to grieve the Holy Spirit. To quench and get in the way of Him moving in this season. In the dream, I was even careful of what I put in my mouth, careful of where I laid my head. Not laying on my sides, not to the right or left but straightforward.

Proverbs 4:25-27 says "*Look straight ahead and fix your eyes on what lies before you. Mark out a straight path for your feet; stay on the safe path. Don't get sidetracked, keep your feet from following evil.*"

Our focus is imperative for fulfilling our mission here on the earth. We are here for reasons greater than we can comprehend with our human minds. What God is doing in us is larger than life, and because of the weight of His glory, we not only need to focus on what's going on spiritually, but our physical bodies need to be strong with healthy eating, drinking, and exercise. There's no use having a mission from God and we can't give it one hundred percent because we didn't take care of our temples, the instruments He gave us to do the job.

Our bodies are the temples of the Holy Spirit. The enemy wants us to abort, to grieve the Holy Spirit, but we are choosing to look straight ahead to the path He has set before us. That basically sums up the understanding I received from the dream. I pray its meaning speaks to you as it spoke to me. Pregnancy can be scary and the contractions painful, but we are graced to push out what He has purposed in us. The earth is contracting. It is painful to see the famine in the land. But we can't allow the rocks to cry out in our place. We are equipped and chosen to cry loud and not hold back. Committed to the great commission.

I pray we are ready and willing to do all that is required to do our part in building the Kingdom of God. Amen and Amen.

SATURDAY, AUGUST 22, 2020

I was invited to share at an international seminar over the web for "Kingdom Biz Ladies Network" (KBL) based in Nigeria. The network is a movement committed to raising God-chasing, impact-driven ladies. They facilitate, inspire, connect, and help to develop skills for ladies in business. I shared about my partnership with our beloved Holy Spirit and how I've only had successes in my career because of God.

It is quite powerful to be a woman of prayer in the workplace. No matter the challenges we face, including Jesus in all our decision-making, inquiring of the Lord about our businesses, ministries, careers, and projects. All of that is so important so that we stay in His will and fulfill His plans for our lives. It is when we attempt to be a boss over everything and exclude Him from the plans that things go badly. I have so many work stories and miracles that took place because of my walk with Jesus. Knowing that we are glory carriers, no matter the arena, we must remember that He is with us. Hallelujah!

I shared my testimony and experiences with the network, letting them know that since I've opened my heart to Jesus to have His way, He sometimes gives me dreams, and I look for opportunities to share the love of Jesus.

I had a dream the night before of someone getting healed of migraines. When I finished presenting, I asked them if anyone had that migraine. I wasn't sure how it would be received to offer prayer, but I mustered up courage to just ask. There was a lady who said it was her who had the issue, that she's suffered from it for a long time. Her head and ear were currently in pain at a level five since the beginning of the presentation. So, I began praying with her, and the other ladies looked on with curiosity. The lady said the pain immediately went away. This was unexpected for all of us; this was a business seminar, and here Jesus showed up and was healing and proving to us that we have to include Him in every area just like this. It was a beautiful experience, and we all felt encouraged to continue to put God first in our careers and allow Him to show up and move in His own way.

At the end of the KBL seminar, I immediately joined our Spirit Lifestyle class. My husband had started it up because the seminar timing was overlapping. I joined and shared the miracle that just took place during the seminar. Everyone was so excited and encouraged, and we started to pray for more deliverances to happen. We were keeping in mind that this is the normal supernatural Christian life. This should be our norm to see deliverance, healings, and breakthroughs like in the book of Acts. One of the new members of the class asked for prayer for high blood pressure, heart palpitations, and gastrointestinal issues. She was in pain at a level six. We all stood in agreement to pray for her. The pain dropped to a "two." She felt something was leaving her. We continued to pray and encouraged her with things to renounce and break agreements with. She then told us the pain dropped to a zero. Glory to Jesus forever! She was so happy, and we all celebrated together.

It is so amazing. Some of the people who joined these sessions just weeks ago are now encouraged to step out in faith to pray for others. That's exactly the effect intended. We are all commissioned. See a testimony below from the lady we prayed for during the SL Session. She wanted me to share what God has done for her.

Testimony

I would like to give God praise as I share my testimony. I joined the class with Dameon and Elisha on Saturday and received prayer for pain which went away during the prayer. I later received words of wisdom and encouragement from Elisha. While she was sharing with me about how we are sometimes oppressed by demonic forces, and as I received the word, I began feeling relief from heaviness in my stomach. Elisha prayed for me, commanding

spirits causing the heaviness, heart palpitations, insomnia, and high blood pressure to leave. As she prayed, I began to vomit. Afterwards, the heaviness was gone, and the palpitations also left. I felt stronger and free. We prayed for complete healing and deliverance from anything out of alignment in my body, and as time goes on, I will continue to share of God's awesome power. I give God praise for His miraculous touch and for using Elisha to minister to me. I look forward to what God will do through me to help others.I thank our Jesus.

~*Chanelle.* Canada.

TUESDAY, AUGUST 25, 2020

A dear sister and friend of mine called for prayer because she'd been having aches and pains suddenly in her back. She thought it unusual because she's always very active throughout the day and has never had issues like that before. She's a woman of faith and God uses her often to minister to others in so many ways. I believe this was a spiritual attack. This happens sometimes. The enemy tries to use things to distract us, to make us worry, to take our focus off ministry and focus on afflictions. She knew exactly what was going on. She called me because she simply wanted me to stand in faith with her faith. It is written in Deuteronomy 32:30, "....one chase a thousand, and two put ten thousand to flight." This is also why working together in unity as the body of Christ is so powerful. We already have the victory through Jesus. Standing in agreement with each other for the same cause—the cause of Christ—an explosion happens and our cities, regions, and the world would be impacted. So, Jesus met us over the phone call as I prayed for this dear sister. I spoke to her muscles, surrounding tissues, and for the spirit of pain to leave. I then spoke to a pinched nerve to be released...She noticed as I prayed for the pinched nerve that the pain immediately left. We prayed until all the symptoms were gone. She tested it out a few times and noticed everything was better. We give glory to Jesus! She shared with me in her words her experience during the prayer.

Testimony

I had been experiencing stiffness and pain in my upper back, between my shoulder blades. It was a dull pain that became more prominent when I would turn my head or move my body while I was lying in bed. I called Elisha, and she began praying for me. She heard the Holy Spirit specifically say, "pinched nerve," and once she called it out, I received immediate relief. After, there was a little stiffness, and we went back into prayer, and the stiffness was gone! I thank God for His healing power through Jesus' blood. I also thank God for using Elisha and for her obedience, boldness, and her authority in the Spirit.

~*Joselyn*. Michigan.

PRAYER AND ACTIVATION:

I'm so proud of God, and I want Him to be proud of me. Ways to show that we are proud of Him include openly testifying of His goodness and not being ashamed. We must not be concerned about what people think, but remember we are here for reasons greater than we think. If you want to be strengthened in that area, let's pray about it. Let's talk to the Father together:

Dear Heavenly Father,

Thank You for being who You are and for giving us access to power. Because of what Jesus did for us, we have the Comforter to lead us and guide us on this journey (John 16:7). Help me to not be ashamed of the gospel, to share openly, and freely give as You've given to me (Romans 1:16).
Make me like a tree of righteousness, well-watered and producing good fruit. I want to walk in Your supernatural insight, wisdom, knowledge, and comprehension. I want to make You proud, to be the best possible version of myself as Your ambassador (2 Corinthians 5:20).
My mind is blessed, and I am receiving downloads of information to live a glorious life. I am a participant in the divine experience, I walk in Your Word. I stand on it, and it comes alive in me (Hebrews 4:12).
I'm walking in newness and have become Your living tabernacle. I'm so proud to have You and long to unveil Your characteristics, glory, wisdom, grace, and love. Use me to dispense miracles. It is an honor to yield my life in service to Your works.
In Jesus' name. Amen.

Chapter Nine

SEPTEMBER MIRACLES

"And my speech and my preaching were not with persuasive words of human wisdom, but in demonstration of the Spirit and of power, that your faith should not be in the wisdom of men but in the power of God." 1 Corinthians 2:4–5

Demonstration of God's power signifies the extraordinary God we serve, and His miracles should be ordinary for us. My confidence is not in my own wisdom or ability to speak. This is what Paul shared about. I didn't understand the significance of this passage until I had an encounter with the Holy Spirit myself, and I moved out of His way so that He could lead and guide. Reading the Word, chewing on it, meditating on it, and truly falling in love with it is also important. But the move of God happens when we stand on the Word, believe it, live it, apply it, and step out in faith to present opportunities for Him to move. It pleases God to use us, and I vow to give God permission to love others through me. Demonstration!

FRIDAY, SEPTEMBER 4, 2020

I mentioned Pastor Ben and shared his wonderful testimony in Chapter 7. I had the opportunity to pray with his wife, Agnes, as well. She suddenly was dealing with pains in her body. She's a Christian minister and spends the majority of her day sharing Jesus, offering prayers in her village, passing out food and supplies, and teaching the villagers' children scriptures. She reached out to me asking for prayers for a few issues she'd been going through, that was also taking away her sleep. She could not turn her head nor enjoy eating because of stomach pains. We finally were able to find a mutual time to pray today over the phone. She sounded so heavy at first. It was obvious she was exhausted from the issues and lack of rest. I shared encouraging words and scriptures with her on how I knew God wants her to be free from this, and then we prayed. She said her pain levels were at eight out of ten. Then I started to speak to her body, commanding the spirit of pain to leave in Jesus' name. The pains dropped to a three after a while, and we gave glory to Jesus. I heard excitement returning to her voice.

Our Helper is always nearby. Jesus is always near, and she felt a breakthrough happening. We went back into prayer and commanded all the pain to *leave now* and go straight to the feet of Jesus to be dealt with as He desires. Jesus did a complete work at the cross. I encouraged her that He doesn't do things halfway. He is the same today, yesterday, and forever. I asked her to test it out. She said she felt as if a heaviness was lifted off her. Hallelujah! She said the pain was a zero, and we worshiped our healer together. Glory to Jesus forever! He is so wonderful! I asked her to share her testimony; these are her words.

Testimony

Beloved of God, I thank God for healing me today. I prayed with my sister, Elisha. Distance did not hinder God's healing power to reach me. I have been having sharp neck pains (eight out of ten on a pain scale) on my left side for a month now, I could not move it. Also, stomach pains (six out of ten pain). But after praying with my sister, God has healed me in Jesus' name with zero pain. Amen and amen! It was difficult to sleep, but tonight I will sleep like a baby. I am very grateful to God! I am very grateful to God for hearing your beautiful voice today, my sister Elisha. Your voice is also medicine to people.

~*Agnes.* Uganda.

Jesus is the best example of living, walking, and operating in the power of God. He gave us many examples. Even how to approach praying. We find several times in Scripture Jesus stepping away to have private time with God. He would rise early according to Mark 1:35: "*Before daybreak the next morning, Jesus got up and went out to an isolated place to pray.*" So much ministry needed to be done! Whenever everyone else finally woke up, they went looking for Jesus. Verse 36-37 says, "*Later Simon and the others went out to find him. When they found him, they said, 'Everyone is looking for you.'*"

But Jesus had been spending much needed time with the Father. Getting direction and hearing His heart. Verse 38 says, "*But Jesus replied, 'We must go on to other towns as well, and I will preach to them, too. That is why I came.'*" It was obvious that Jesus knew where He was to go next—prayer will do just that. God gives us directions and points us to the paths He wants us to take. It doesn't matter if people around us understand. The disciples could have gotten impatient with Jesus. He spent all this time in prayer, and when they finally found Him, they wanted Him to come along with them, but He headed in another direction.

Verse 39 says, "*So he traveled throughout the region of Galilee, preaching in the synagogues and casting out demons.*" We can easily get caught up in what we feel we need to do, like ministry and other things we feel are right. But we must remember the importance of getting direction from God in all things. Spending time with God in solitude like Jesus did, having individual worship and prayer.

Verse 40-42 says, "*A man with leprosy came and knelt in front of Jesus, begging to be healed. 'If you are willing, you can heal me and make me clean,' he said. Moved with compassion, Jesus reached out and touched him. 'I am willing,' he said. 'Be healed!' Instantly the leprosy disappeared, and the man was healed.*"

Jesus was empowered with prayer, and moved and demonstrated God's love in that moment. It was instant. Jesus didn't have to spend hours, days, weeks, or months trying to get these results. He had spent hours with God to get these types of instant results when He spoke healing over people. We can have this effect on people around us. Time is the cost—the time we spend alone in the secret place, according to Psalms 91.

SATURDAY, SEPTEMBER 9, 2020

During our Saturday Zoom session, we shared on having faith for healing. We also prayed for God to move supernaturally for us individually, to show us things that we've forgotten that need to be given to Him through prayer. We agreed on how it starts with faith the size of a mustard seed.

Jesus taught on this in Mark 4:30-32, "*Jesus said, "How can I describe the Kingdom of God? What story should I use to illustrate it? It is like a mustard seed planted in the ground. It is the smallest of all seeds, but it becomes the largest of all garden plants; it grows long branches, and birds can make nests in its shade.*" It is beyond the human mind to conceive all that's within the tiny seed. All of God's wonderful works are potentially in it. Those who have an interest in growing plants can understand the gardening process! It takes time and care, and it will grow. Like planting seeds of faith and accomplishing huge things, over and over, growing so large and producing fruits. The beautiful thing about fruit is anyone who comes to the tree can see the fruit and eat from its produce. The tree also gives shade to others as an added benefit.

The Kingdom of God grows and grows, and there are so many people we cross paths with that need spiritual nourishment, relief from weights and shade from the hot sun. A child of God's mission is to share and keep the growing of the tree's going, telling of the goodness of Jesus. Once we've shared, others can grab it and believe it. Now Proverbs 30:5 can be seen. "*Every promise from the faithful God is pure and proves to be true. He is an all-encompassing shield of protection for all who run to hide in Him.*

As we started prayer during the session, several of us were reminded of things that were forgotten or purposely hidden away due to trauma or just because it happened so long ago. We stood in faith, like James 2:20. Faith is not just agreeing with something; it is also acting on it. By faith, we went before the throne of God with repenting hearts and opened ourselves to be completely washed.

God knows the things that have been sent to oppress and attack. One of the ladies had a dream about her finances a long time ago and didn't think much of it until this session. She was able to address what she saw in that dream. As she renounced the spiritual darkness, she started to experience deliverance and breakthrough. Every deliverance is different; not everyone reacts the same way. But as a spirit was obviously leaving out of her, she coughed and purged.

From her updates after prayer, she has noticed good changes in her finances, finally able to buy a new home and job opportunities. Her testimony all the way from South Africa will follow this scripture. I believe that every believer who gives their life to doing the will of God will grow stronger in every way. Day by day and step by step, it is a process. Psalm 1 says,

"Oh, the joys of those who do not follow the advice of the wicked, or stand around with sinners, or join in with mockers. But they delight in the law of the Lord, meditating on it day and night. They are like trees planted along the riverbank, bearing fruit each season. Their leaves never wither, and they prosper in all they do. But not the wicked! They are like worthless chaff, scattered by the wind. They will be condemned at the time of judgment. Sinners will have no place among the godly. For the Lord watches over the path of the godly, but the path of the wicked leads to destruction."

Testimony

God is so, so good. While you prayed, I agreed and began praying in tongues, and I also put on Fire prophetic music. When you commanded the spirits to go in Jesus' name, I began vomiting, and it happened several times.
I agree that the Lord delivered me from dark spirits as well. After ending our session, I just felt so much lighter and just felt the urge to pray over our finances as the Holy Spirit reminded me instantly about a dream I had last year about this filthy-looking man. His clothes were dirty, and his hair was long and full of dirt. He

came after me and my husband in the dream, demanding us to give him money.

My husband did not want to give it to him and out of fear and wanting him to leave, I told my husband to give him the money. Before I could see if my husband did give him the money, the scene changed into where it looks as if a war took place in this city.

Every building was destroyed, and I remember several people standing on our side and a prophet from the United States who I was connected to a few years ago on social media. This same dirty man appeared, and the prophet picked a building and lifted it above his head and quoted Psalm 24, saying "Lift up your heads all ye gates and be ye lifted up" and this dirty man instantly fell down and seemed very scared for this prophet. So, the Holy Spirit told me to begin praying against this demon stealing our money and against holes in our purses and bank accounts.

~*Judene.* South Africa.

PRAYER FORMULA

Becoming a Spirit Lifestyle coach has, in a way, required more time to my already-loaded schedule. Did I mention that schools are closed, and the kids are home schooling until further notice over Zoom with their teachers right now? I'm monitoring everything to make sure they stay on track with assignments. We're adjusting to everyone being at home at the same time all day. I'm called on a whole lot more than usual. "Mom, help me with this!" "Mom, I'm hungry again." "Mom, my computer is freezing." "Mom, I want a snack." "Mom, I don't understand how to do this math problem."

I love my children, don't get me wrong, but I feel overwhelmed at times. Not to mention the cooking, cleaning, and organizing that I do in between. So, it has been tough to balance working from home and trying to be the support for everyone else. It seems my husband's business has gotten even busier during this time also, that's a happy problem really. I know God put it on my heart to become a coach—there's no question about it. But I want to make sure I'm doing this the right way. So, I've been talking to Jesus about that and allowing Him to move things around. He's really been opening my eyes to understanding prayer in the middle of all this. How to make necessary adjustments when needed. What used to work before probably won't work right now. We are all on different schedules during different seasons.

Jesus shows us how to pray, how to listen—how to do *everything*. I had to redesign my schedule to make sure that I was making time for earnest prayer. That's so important to me. I can feel the void when I'm not praying like I should. We can get so busy with life sometimes and forget how to incorporate prayer. I want my life to mirror the prayer habits that Jesus displayed. He regularly went to communicate with the Father. Jesus shows us how He made this a priority for life, not just when things were going wrong. It was a part of His everyday walk. I've heard the saying, "If I wait until I'm in trouble to pray, I'm in BIG trouble."

One day while driving in my car, I asked God to give me something that I can understand when it comes to prayer, anything He would want to show me. We should make a habit of doing this, it is fun. A formula came to mind. Ohm's Law (I x R = V). I was confused. This is a formula I use in electrical engineering. I wondered, "Why did this formula drop in my mind?" I continued to pray and ask God why.

Then I heard, "Think about it." The formula was before me in its original meaning, the electrical terms being "I" (current) x "R" (resistance) = "V" (voltage). "Current" is the rate of flow of electrical charge in a circuit, "resistance" is a measure of the opposition to current flow, and "voltage" is the pressure from an electrical circuit's power source.

God showed me how spiritually, "I" is intercession, and if we pray extra, putting more time in, this will bypass the "R," resistance, which comes in life. Resistance is like a barrier sent to cause delay, slow down progress, or cause limitations. Things like bloodline curses, sickness, oppression, depressions, financial restraints, relationship problems and anything the enemy uses to try to hurt us.

But if we readjust the calculations of how much intercession, how much time we spend building up strength and momentum while talking to the Father, we will burst past the resistance, totally breaking the strongholds down, gaining the victorious results that Heaven wants us to possess!

This formula changed my prayers forever. Unbelievably I asked while driving and this download came. This is what I mean by adjusting. We have to be open to pray all day, anywhere, anytime. Our relationship with God should evolve into a perpetual prayer position. God gives us things we can relate to and meets us where we are so that we can understand.

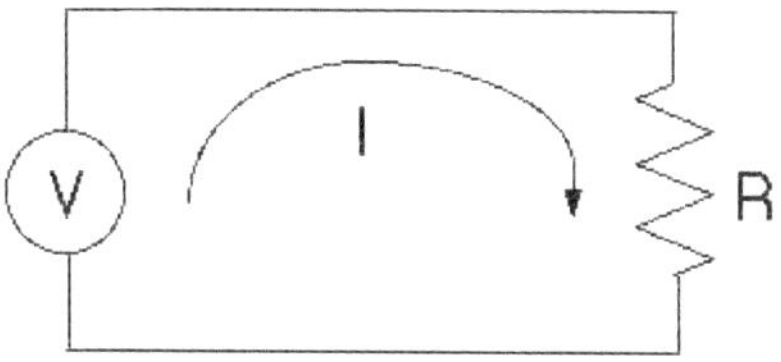

Ohm's Law or Prayer Formula

Jesus didn't fight with demons for hours, tarrying for them to go. He spent hours with God and minutes with men. In Luke 5:13-14, Jesus reached out and touched the leper and said, *"I am willing...Be healed! And instantly the leprosy disappeared."* Instantly, the leprous sores were healed, and his skin became smooth. Jesus, the Lord of the Sabbath, healed a man who had been unable to walk for thirty-eight years (John 5:1-18). Jesus told the lame man to pick up his bed and walk. The Sabbath rule-enforcers were waiting to pounce. Sabbath enforcers didn't care that a man who had been crippled for thirty-eight years had been healed. It is written all through the scriptures: instant results, but blind so-called believers, unable to see the magnificent and spectacular miracles that were occurring everywhere Jesus went.

Can we master this prayer formula? Master the skill of praying? Any new skill requires resolve and practice, including our devotional life.

In different seasons of life, we will find different ways of engaging with God in our devotions. It helped that I could adjust with the change of season. I had to be flexible, not complaining that my schedule was interrupted. I have little kids, and sometimes things don't work out as planned. Having a plan, A, B, and C for devotional times is a good idea. Think it over. How can it be done? Keep it in your back pocket for when adjustments are needed.

Hey, a full-time wife and mom, who works long hours, has to go with the flow! If something is not working, flip through the plans. An example of plan A would be getting up hours before everyone else wakes to pray and have some quiet time, then don't stop there, continue walking with God all day. Plan B could be to set an alarm for short, targeted intentional prayers throughout the day while walking with God. Plan C could be to sleep in because your tired, but pray when you first wake, pray while taking a run at the gym, and pray before bed, but of course walking with the Lord all day. The goal is to have a plan until it is second nature and becomes a continuous conversation between friends. The possibilities are endless. The key is to find what works for you. What matters is making prayer the norm.

Taking these extra steps has deepened my relationship and security in God. Literally watching my prayers transform things, elevating my faith, interceding for my family, friends, coworkers, neighbors, and complete strangers. Intercession is the act of asking God for help on behalf of others, we pray for others until they can pray for themselves. Intercessors do for others what they can't do until they can.

I can hear the song they used to sing when I was a little girl in church, "Somebody prayed for me, / had me on their mind, / took the time and prayed for me. / I'm so glad they prayed, / I'm so glad they prayed, / I'm so glad they prayed for me."

Prayer works if we take that step of faith to give it a try and just watch what God does. Yes, it takes discipline and our precious time, but I believe miracles are possible every time we go to God in prayer. When we believe something, it shows in our actions and sacrifices.

PRAYER AND ACTIVATION:

God speaks to us right where we are and can use us right where we are. Sometimes we may feel the pressure of trying to meet a certain standard. That's a waste of time! We should never compare or judge who God will use or how He will go about doing it. I love how Paul said that his preaching was not with persuasive words, but in demonstration of power, so that people would not look to men's wisdom but have faith in God. If you are feeling the pressure of trying to fit a mold formed by men, let that go now. Let's talk to the Father together about it:

Dear Heavenly Father,

Thank You that you have a calling for each of us (Jeremiah 29:11). That there are no "big I's" or "little you's" in Your Kingdom (Romans 2:11). Thank You that we don't have to compete or try to fit a mold formed by men.

I don't have excellent speech, I'm not the smartest in the world, but You are, and I function in Your excellence (1 Corinthians 2:1). Your wisdom and revelations touch the heart of men. All degrees and certifications in the world, although good, are without power. I choose to depend on You rather than the wisdom of men (1 Corinthians 2:5).

I live in the full advantage of all that's available to me in Christ. I live beyond the limitations of the human mind. I am what You say I am, and I will do what You say I will do. If You guide me, I'm strong and able to walk and operate in truth (John 3:21). Your divine life emits from me as I stand on Your words and deeds. I will forever be a student and lover of Your Word.

Thank You for giving me revelation and understanding to share in ways

that will draw people to You. I yield to Your way of doing things and break loose from the opinion of others.
In Jesus' name. Amen.

Chapter Ten

OCTOBER MIRACLES

"I tell you the truth, anyone who believes in me will do the same works I have done, and even greater works, because I am going to be with the Father!" John 14:12

SATURDAY, OCTOBER 3, 2020

I shared with our Saturday session a dream I had. The words "sweet communication" stood out to me. The dream was about the physical heart and how important it is in pumping blood to the rest of the entire body. How the heart is a muscle always working to keep everything circulating and communicating. Every system in the body depends on the heart pumping the blood through. It is a miracle of God how it takes less than sixty seconds for the heart to pump blood to every cell throughout the body.

My mother's name is Deborah, she works in the cardiac department of a hospital. She studies and examines hearts all day. The heart is her favorite thing. She absolutely loves it and how it functions. She was in my dream also as we explained to a group of people the relativity of the heart and our communication with God. I loved the fact that as I was sharing with a group of people, I had a heart specialist right there with me. I didn't have all the answers, but she did, so in the dream, there was a comfort in knowing the support system that I had. It is like on our journeys now with Jesus. We don't have all the answers, but He does. He specializes in the conditions of our heart. The heart of the matter depends on the matter of our hearts. We need our hearts to be clean. He knows us from the inside out and will teach us how to do it. We can't hide anything. If the heart stops beating and pumping blood to the rest of the body, there's a break in circulation, which causes big problems. The last thing we need is clogged valves. One by one, every organ in the body starts to shut down and fail. Overall, death occurs within minutes. We can't afford to have our line of communication broken with our heart specialist. There must be a constant circulation from the heart, without a timeout, to ensure proper functionality. It says in 1 Thessalonians 5:16-18, "*Always be joyful. Never stop praying. Be thankful in all circumstances, for this is God's will for you who belong to Christ Jesus.*"

Jesus is the true vine; the life blood flows through Him. Obeying 1 Thessalonians 5:16-18 would help us to not fluctuate with our emotions or circumstances. It will take work sometimes, but God is telling us to be joyful, never stop praying, and be thankful, even if it goes against what we are feeling in that moment. Obedience will help us to see from a new perspective. The limitations in our mind, making us feel like the present is our reality, but it is not, and that will soon fade away.

We realize that Jesus never fails. That we must communicate constantly with Him. It is impossible to be on our knees in prayer twenty-four hours a day. But we can always keep a praying attitude. If we don't, it is as if the heart slows down and does not pump the blood as needed, opening doors to possible premature disconnection and dysfunction in our lives. Like any relationship, communication is a requirement for health and to stay strong. Every part of our being (spirit, soul, body) can be whole through Him. Some people are experiencing spiritual cardiac arrest and not understanding that connection to the Father, fulfilling 1 Thessalonians 5:17 (pray without ceasing), is how to recover from spiritual and physical brokenness. Spiritual death leads to physical death. The only way to live whole and free is with sweet communication with the Father.

Joshua 1:8-9 says, "*Study this Book of Instruction continually. Meditate on it day and night so you will be sure to obey everything written in it. Only then will you prosper and succeed in all you do. This is my command—be strong and courageous! Do not be afraid or discouraged. For the Lord your God is with you wherever you go.*"

There it is again: meditating day and night, and only then will we prosper. This is the answer to many questions. It is possible to succeed in all we do if we meditate on it until its truth finds us by asking the Lord to help us understand, opening our minds, and allowing it to melt in our hearts. Then we speak it out from our heart; that's what causes the Kingdom realities to manifest in our lives. Some think prosperity comes with popularity, power, or influential contacts. God shows us what works. Be courageous, be strong, obey God, and constantly meditate on the Word of God.

TUESDAY, OCTOBER 13, 2020

I was Facetiming with my auntie Pamela and "sister cousin" Brittani (sister cousin is the name I use for all my girl cousins; it's like we are sisters. And I have so much respect for my aunts and uncles who are like bonus parents.) They're from Atlanta, Georgia. We were catching up and checking on each other. My auntie Pamela is the one who, although she always lived out of state, would call and check on me during my teen years. I had a landline in my room, and she would randomly make efforts to see how I was getting along. She checked on my spirit and would not let me retract into my introverted emotional cave. All through high school, she kept up with me and would encourage me. I didn't understand how much I needed those talks back then. But now looking back, I needed her, and I'm so thankful to God for the time she invested in me.

So, this was one of those calls, she has not stopped even though I'm married and have children of my own now. To this day, I pick up the phone and hear her voice say, "Hey girl, what's going on?" I love every bit of it. We shared testimonies of what God had been doing in our lives. So much good happening in the middle of a pandemic, and we are thankful. God is adding to the family, Brittani is expecting her first child and God opened doors for her to purchase a new home.

We continued to share, and I noticed Brittani was holding her head a certain way. She told me that she just went to the doctor because she's been having pain in her neck. The doctor said she somehow sprained her neck. She hadn't been able to turn her head for a week and was a bit concerned because there was so much work approaching where she would need to move things around without limitations. I was going to ask if we could pray, but as I was thinking it, my auntie said, "Let's pray now for the pain to leave." She took the words right out of my mouth.

We started to pray and stand in agreement for her neck to be healed, to remove the stiffness, to touch the tissues, her spine, the vertebrae, muscles, and nerves, all of it. We commanded for all the pain to leave in Jesus' name. Immediately after we asked her to test it out. She was lying on the couch. Then she sat up and proceeded to turn her neck fully. She said there's no pain! Wow! Amazing God! We all raised our voices in shock and amazement. We celebrated and continued sharing together in that beautiful moment. It is so exciting to walk in our norm with Jesus. For the believer's this is the normal supernatural Christian life. I'm so happy for my family, and I love them so much.

My "sister cousin" Brittani and Auntie Pam. Georgia.

WEDNESDAY, OCTOBER 14, 2020

I was invited to speak for an organization over Zoom called "TechKeyz." It is a group of young people from all walks of life who support one another and share ways to use the resources around them to excel in following their dreams, starting businesses, finishing school, supporting family, and ministry. I wanted to inspire them to go after their dreams, but to always remember to include God in it. I shared about my career, how God navigated my life, how I gave it all to Him, and it allowed for supernatural things to happen around me. I shared testimonies of how He is watching us and loves us all so much. That He sent Jesus, Jesus being God's expressed will in the earth. That God wants us all to completely receive Him, to partner with the Holy Spirit, to have a real encounter with Jesus.

I walked them through prayers of repentance and offered prayers for any requests. I told them that God can do anything if they open their hearts and let Him in. There was a lady online named Renee from

New Zealand. There was no video, but there was a voice call on her end. She asked for prayer because she was in a lot of pain. I learned later that her video was off because she was not well and forced to lay in the bed during the session. She was in excruciating pain. This was her testimony. She sent an update after this one stating that after our session, God continued to move within her, and she is completely free from pain. Healed through Jesus. The founder of the group sent me this testimony from Renee. See below what she shared in her words.

Testimony

I have been suffering from sciatic nerve damage for years. Probably about seven or eight years, maybe longer. It would hit me, and I would literally be bedridden for weeks! I just learned to live with it. It would only happen two to four times a year, but each time, I would be out of action for weeks. My mum would have to come to my house and take care of my children and, well, me too. Not only did this ailment mess me up physically, but it also tore me up mentally. I am their mother; I should be the one looking after them. I felt incompetent. Useless. Although I knew I'd get better eventually, I was always waiting for the next time it would pop up again and take me out. It was inevitable. Bound to happen again...I couldn't sit down for long periods of time. Thirty minutes at most, if that, and even that was painful. So off to bed I go.

The year 2020 was a great year for me pertaining to this illness. Had niggles here and there, but didn't get to the bedridden stage until October11. It struck me down. Yes, I stayed prayerful. But always submitted to staying in this agony. Oh well, here we go again. Great! Today is October 15, and I woke up the same as yesterday and the day before, and the day before that. In strife. Any tiny movement I made, my nerves would clench, and pain would strike through my body like someone was stabbing me with 1000 nails on my insides. I walked with a crutch because the pain shot down to my legs. If I made any sudden movements, my legs could give way, which they have many times before, and I'd be on the ground crawling and crying trying to get back to my bed. I would not wish this upon anyone! I say this often: I'd rather give birth! At noon on Thursday, New Zealand time, I joined a Zoom meeting with my fellow TechKeyz.

It was a Spirit Lifestyle Course delivered by Mrs. Elisha Brown. I wasn't going to join because I was tired and a little weary from the medication, but the Lord had His way. From the moment Elisha spoke, I was engaged. She had me throwing my hands in the air and screaming at my phone. If I could've gotten up and danced, I would have, but nerve pain—so, no! Towards the end, she asked if anyone needed a prayer. I'm not usually one to ask to be prayed over because I always think someone needs it more than I do. There's always someone whose needs are more than mine!

But today, I felt a push from the Lord to speak up. He said, "Tell this woman that I have placed right here in your presence, the pain you're in. She is willing to call Me into your body to heal you! SPEAK!" (Or type in this instance.) So, I did. I told her what I was suffering from, and she asked me what my pain level was. I said, "a ten." She spoke over my illness—no, she SHOUTED over my illness and rebuked it from my body.

My body started to shake and tremble. Tears were streaming down my face onto my pillow. I couldn't control it. I could not sit up normally out of the bed, I had to move in particular ways so my nerves would not pinch. It would take me five minutes just to sit up! Well, I SAT RIGHT ON UP!!!!! WHAAAATTTT?! Pain was still there, but declining rapidly to about a five...then, wait—THEN I STOOD UP UNASSISTED AND WALKED!

I couldn't walk without my crutch. I really couldn't! I walked into my lounge in hysterics! My body was shivering at this point, and I felt this overwhelming power flowing through my entire body. My breathing was heavy and swift. Tears were falling. The pain was literally being shaken out of me! I have never experienced anything like this. I had to get in the shower and warm up because I was freezing and almost hyperventilating! Usually, even getting in the shower proved difficult for me. But not today! I'm sitting here, SITTING (not lying down), on Thursday afternoon, 3:09 p.m. New Zealand time, still in awe of what I have just experienced! Jesus, the healing of Jesus, the Miracle Worker! People who know me and have seen me with this debilitating pain that takes over my body know how bad it can be. I don't want to say I can't believe because I DO BELIEVE IT! God knew I needed to be in that Zoom meeting, and I thank Him for giving me the courage to speak out and ask, for once, for a prayer of healing.

So, I thank Elisha Brown for allowing God to use her. What she said about me is all true. Totally blew my mind! I have been a spiritual being from a very young age. Just wasn't sure on how to "use" it, so I'd often try and forget about it. I will not take that for granted. I'm still growing in my journey with the Lord, and I'm excited to see where He is going to take me. Hallelujah!

I know sometimes you must let people intercede on your behalf. Today was a true testimony of that! All my prayers are for other people, and there's nothing wrong with that, right? But okay, what about me? Yeah, I ask the Lord to do things in my life, but then I say, "I must take the pain so no one else will suffer from it, then so be it!"

No! No more sickness, no more pain! Not for me, not for anyone! It doesn't belong here. I will not allow it. My pain is now a "one." I can move with ease. I can walk without fear of falling. I can sit for longer, and I will be going back to work Monday! All in one evening, God healed my body! And for that I am and will be forever grateful! All glory to the highest! Thank You Father! This is my testimony.
Renee and her sons. New Zealand.

WEDNESDAY, OCTOBER 21, 2020

I took a modeling commercial job for an automotive company. I got dressed, went to take a COVID test (which was required to be on set), and took the negative results to the set. They checked me in once I arrived and showed me to the talent motor home where I waited for the wardrobe stylist to inform me of what I was wearing for the first scene. I sat there and watched out the window as the setup crew was changing some props around and working on what footage would be captured first.

Normally when this happens, I'll check messages and respond to engineering emails, or read a nice book, or study scriptures. I learned from experience to bring options to set because the hours can fluctuate, and if you have multiple jobs like me, you can work on one while having down time with the other.

I noticed I had a message in my inbox from a lady requesting prayer for sciatic nerve pain. She saw Renee's testimony from New Zealand, how God healed her, and was thinking she would like that to happen for her too. I responded to her saying that I was on break for a few minutes and could call right then if she was available. She responded immediately that she was available, so I called her, and we introduced ourselves officially. She gave me a little background on her issue. She'd been off work for five years and could barely do regular activities. She told me her right leg was the most painful. She had been praying, but so far, the issue remained.

I encouraged her and shared some scriptures (Psalms 103:2-3; Jeremiah 30:17; Isaiah 53:5; Mark 11:25) and I told her how, "*The Lord is merciful and gracious, slow to anger, and plenteous in mercy*" (Psalms 103:8). We discussed how healing is universal. It is a privilege, and an act of God's mercy given in forgiveness. I told her just like the scripture says in Psalms 103:1-3, God forgives *all* iniquities, and He heals *all* diseases. When we read how He "forgives all," it is just as eternal as "heals all." Just like it happened for Renee in New Zealand, it can happen for her.

She received the words I shared in faith. Then we started to pray with those same scriptures. I commanded the pain to leave and report to the feet of Jesus, to be dealt with as He desires. I then asked her to test it out to see if she could locate the pain. She tested it out and couldn't find pain. That was wonderful! She said she would get back with me after checking out things she couldn't do like exercise or stand for long periods of time.

During the prayer, she was standing, and was surprised that she wasn't in pain. Normally simply standing or pressure on her legs would cause an issue. So, we thanked God for all He was doing and ended the call. I was still on break in the motor home. Our conversation was short, straight to the point and sweet. Soon after that call ended, I was called to set to start shooting footage for the commercial. That was excellent timing! God's doing for sure.

A few days passed and I heard back from her. She literally tried several things to see if the pain was truly gone. She said she felt great and had not felt that good in a while. She was doing things she hadn't been able to do. God is so awesome. Hallelujah! See her testimony below. These are her words.

Testimony

I was reading a testimony on Elisha's page (about sciatic nerve damage). I was in pain too; it caught my attention because it was something I was experiencing (I could not stand nor sit for long periods of time). I messaged Elisha for prayer to touch and agree for my healing, we prayed, and I received my healing that day. I got on the treadmill the same day and felt no pain. I've been doing daily activities for days with no pain. I haven't felt this good in a while, glory be to God. Thanks, my sister, for praying with me. Thank You, Jesus, for complete healing.

Julia Early, Michigan.

PRAYER AND ACTIVATION:

If you are experiencing sciatic pain, or any other types of issues in your body, let's talk to the Father together and give it to Him now. Pray this prayer and repeat it as often as you want, believe in healing.

Dear Heavenly Father,

I know that You love me, and it is not Your will for me to have pain, sicknesses, or issues. I invite the Holy Spirit to come and reveal the root of where this issue has come from, the door that was opened. I repent for coming into agreement with any of it. If I opened the door, I repent for those actions and I completely let go. I forgive myself and anyone else who may have wronged me (Mark 11:25).
I confess with my mouth the Lord Jesus. I believe in my heart that You raised Him from the dead that I might be saved, healed, and delivered (Romans 10:9-10). I thank You, Jesus, for saving me from sin and delivering me from sickness. Replace my blood with Yours.
I renounce the spirit of darkness (call out the symptoms you are experiencing).
I renounce unforgiveness, divination, familiar spirits; I renounce fear, etc. I command it to leave me now in the name of Jesus. Every contract, legal bindings, or covenants Satan has used to oppress me, it is now pronounced null and void.
I divorce myself from pain, I divorce myself from oppressions, I divorce myself from all sickness and issues now.
Thank You for filling me and renewing me in every way. I speak restoration, healing, deliverance, freedom to my life now, in Jesus' name. Amen and Amen.

Chapter Eleven

NOVEMBER MIRACLES

"Jesus realized at once that healing power had gone out from him, so he turned around in the crowd and asked, "Who touched my robe?"
Mark 5:30

Sometimes we feel our problems will keep us from God. Time and time again, we can find examples in Scripture showing us that it didn't matter what problem they faced, the love of God was always there. We may feel crowded, up against the wall, cornered, or like the world is against us. It doesn't matter. God is there, and His love is bigger than our circumstances. We should never allow fear or worry to stop us from pressing our way through.

I want to be that person that prays and perseveres to touch Jesus. I want that crazy faith that will cause Him to say, "Who touched my robe?" The lady in Mark 5 must have felt so hopeless. She was weak from her years of suffering but still pressed in. I can't tell you how many times I felt tired or weak, didn't want to pray, didn't feel like it. But when I did and pressed in, I felt Him and the heaviness I was feeling changed.

Getting close to Him is the key. We don't need permission to do that. He is where the healing is. We must come up to where He is and not try to pull Him down to where we are or try to pull the Word of God down to affirm our thinking and ways of living.

Revelations 4:1 says, "*...The voice said, 'Come up here, and I will show you what must happen after this.'*" We must press through to come up where He is. Touching His robe, going before the throne of grace in prayer and expectation, kneeling before the God who sits on the throne and orchestrates everything.

Our lives are not spinning out of control. God will always carry out His plans. The woman who pressed her way to touch His robe not only was healed, but Jesus affirmed her faith. He didn't even know she touched Him until He felt the virtue leave from Him. How interesting is that? I want to surprise Jesus with my faith. This lady had so many years of suffering traded in for a lifetime of peace. The Pharisees in the crowd were just curious, hanging around to spectate. But people like this woman were hungry and desired to touch Jesus and receive His healing power and love, transforming them forever.

THURSDAY, NOVEMBER 15, 2020

Our sons are so playful and full of energy that it makes me envious sometimes! Well, they were playing together like they normally do, and I heard a lot of commotion suddenly. Someone was crying, and I thought: uh oh, what now? I rushed to them to see and started asking questions. They were running and playing roughly as boys sometimes do. Our oldest son, Dameon Jr. (who was ten years old at the time), was being chased by our youngest son Elisha (who was eight years old). Somehow Elisha's arm and back were injured by the door during the chase. Elisha was in tears; he said the pain was great, and it would not stop hurting. This made me nervous. I didn't want to have to go to the hospital in the middle of a pandemic. Hospitals were swamped now with COVID-19 cases, and it is hard to get in. I continued to monitor him and just prepared to go to the hospital. I gave him some pain medicine to hold him over, but it didn't work. It was getting late; he couldn't hold up his arm, so I was thinking maybe it somehow was knocked out the socket. We were preparing to head to the car to go to the emergency room. I was helping with Elisha's coat, being careful to not hurt his lifeless arm. And then Elisha turned to me and said, "Please pray for me mom."

It is like a light bulb went off in my head. I put my bags down and just looked at him. I thought, "why didn't I think to do that?" With all the commotion, my nervousness got the best of me. You see how that can happen so easily? God knows how we feel about our babies, but Satan knows too. I snapped out of it, though, and said, "Of course buddy. Let's pray."

I put my hands on his shoulder and back and spoke to his bones, muscles, joints, and commanded healing in Jesus' name. I told all the pain, soreness, and aches to leave *now* in Jesus' name. We prayed for one minute perhaps, and then I asked him to look for the pain. To try and move that arm. He started to move his arm. Then his eyes got big, bigger, and then even bigger. He just gazed in amazement looking up at me. He told me the pain was gone. He proceeded to test the limitations of his arm. He lifted it over his shoulder and said, "Wait a minute?! Wow, it is really gone mom!"

I just started to laugh and praise God. The boys stood gazing at each other, still trying to figure out what just happened. I asked Elisha what made him think to ask me to pray for him. He said he was thinking of how he knew that Jesus could heal him. That the medicine didn't work, but he knows that Jesus works. Amazing! JESUS WORKS! I'm never going to forget him saying that to me.

The boys went to bed talking about the miracle. They stayed up discussing how they just don't know how God does that. I share testimonies with them all the time, so they've heard it before. But I know from experience, it is nothing like having a miracle for yourself. Everything we've read in the Word of God is true. All we must do is believe, like the woman in Mark 5. Our belief activates miracles (Mark 5:34).

I don't know if I had faith like my son at his age. It is encouraging, and I pray they continue to build on that. I'll continue to share all that I'm seeing and experiencing with them. We can't forget, that's why I journal. I want to make sure that I continue to teach them to go to God, to keep the heart of children even when they grow older. I pray they read my journals when they grow up and remember how the miracles were always happening around us. How the bible inspired me to write my own testimonies. How they can never be the same after experiencing God like this. That they are a part of this journey with the Holy Spirit. I learn from them all the time. Being an adult, sometimes I start trying to figure things out myself. But no, I pray that Matthew 18:3 is fulfilled in all our homes in Jesus' name.

Matthew 18:3 "*Then he said, "I tell you the truth, unless you turn from your sins and become like little children, you will never get into the Kingdom of Heaven."*

We are thankful and blown away at God. We celebrate His sovereignty. I told the kids, including my daughter Salah, that I'm always amazed at God. To just be a son and a daughter of God, focusing on that inheritance. He's our beloved and we are His. What a beautiful mystery! We woke up the next morning talking about Elisha's miracle. He is still completely pain free and has full mobility. That's our Jesus forever!

Me with my boys, Elisha and Dameon Jr., Michigan.

WEDNESDAY, NOVEMBER 18, 2020

I spoke to a lady named Debra from Arkansas. She was having so many issues and couldn't figure out why. For twenty years, she'd been struggling from residual nerve damage. Her knees were bone-to-bone, which also caused her to not be able to walk around much. We discussed how it is God's will for her to be healed. I felt led to talk to her in detail about Matthew 6:14-15, "*If you forgive those who sin against you, your heavenly Father will forgive you. 15 But if you refuse to forgive others, your Father will not forgive your sins.*"

We also talked about Mark 11:25, "*But when you are praying, first forgive anyone you are holding a grudge against, so that your Father in heaven will forgive your sins, too.*"

She started to cry as I told her that she had to let go of any hurt from the past—relationships and disappointments. That it was the Holy Spirit who led us to linger on that topic. She confirmed that it had been very difficult for her to forgive her ex-husband from a twenty-year relationship and painful divorce. We prayed and gave it all to Jesus. She chose to let go and start over afresh so that restoration could begin in her life. She had little to no pain at the end of the prayer and was able to move about her room. I know that as she continues to let go of all the things she carried for so long, God will continue to strengthen her and build her up. Unforgiveness was the door left open for her pain. It was hard for her to see it because she had been let down so much. Honestly, we've all been there in some fashion or time in our lives.

One of my favorite verses is 2 Corinthians 4:18, "*So we don't look at the troubles we can see now; rather, we fix our gaze on things that cannot be seen. For the things we see now will soon be gone, but the things we cannot see will last forever."* This verse has really helped me to understand there's a spirit behind everything. Forgiving someone doesn't mean we are condoning what they did as right, it is showing God that we know we are not in a war against our brothers and sisters. There are principalities at work here. A person going around hurting someone else, seen from spiritual eyes, is a person who was hurt themselves. And this is what Satan goes after—someone who has weaknesses.

We must view all things through our spiritual eyes, through the eyes of our Spirit, through the eyes of faith. A person who looks at things in the natural is motivated by those things; carnal things will get a reaction out of this person. On the flip side, the person who does not focus on what is seen is motivated by the unseen, the Spirit behind everything. This can keep people sick for a long time. Smith Wigglesworth said, "I'm not moved by what I see. I'm not moved by what I feel. I'm moved only by what I believe." We can't see belief, but we can act and look sickness dead in the face and say, "I will not stop praying to be free and healed."

Matthew 6:22 says, *"Your eye is like a lamp that provides light for your body. When your eye is healthy, your whole body is filled with light."* If your heart is unclouded, the light floods in! We must pray for good spiritual vision. To see clearly what God wants us to do and to see the world from His point of view. Jesus was on the cross, forgiving them, for they knew not what they were doing.

Debra from Arkansas learned that she had to forgive like Jesus did. Her prayers were hindered and unforgiveness was disconnecting her from eternal life. The pain melted away as her eyes were illuminated with revelation and light, no more being clogged up with unforgiveness.

Over the past few days, she sent me several messages. The day after prayer, she said "I am pain-free." The day after that she said, "Still feeling good." God is truly amazing, and I'm so happy she is finally free and can fully be restored to health. Twenty years of pain because of bitterness, grudges, resentment, and exhaustion. Jesus wants for us all to be whole, healed, and set free. To see finally and believe that God is working everything out according to His Word.

MONDAY, NOVEMBER 23, 2020

Today was a beautiful day, full of prayer and receiving wonderful testimonies. I spoke with one of my sister cousins (as mentioned previously my cousins are like sisters to me). We were talking about work, just catching up on family stuff like we normally do. She's been working at her church, serving the community. She then told me that she's been suffering from a painful knee. Her knee popped some months ago, and she's been trying to treat it, just trying to be patient as it heals.

She tried everything, but the swelling just would not go down. She's been wearing a knee brace to support. This has been a tough challenge for her, trying to get the swelling down, and the pain so consistent and not appearing to get any better. I asked her if we could pray about it since we were already on the phone. To just give it to the Father, all these things that she just mentioned that she'd been facing. She agreed and we prayed in faith.

I reminded her of Matthew 18:18, "*I tell you the truth, whatever you forbid on earth will be forbidden in heaven, and whatever you permit on earth will be permitted in heaven.*" We commanded the pain to go and report to Jesus. We also told the swelling to get lost completely in Jesus' name. We prayed for a few minutes, and then I asked her to test it out. She could hardly tell with the brace on, so I asked her to take it off so we could get a real clear picture if anything was happening. She removed the brace and noticed immediately that the swelling was gone, and her knee felt great. She was moving it around and walking on it, all while praising God over and over and over. We both were shocked and so happy. What a celebration we had over the phone. It was awesome! There's no distance in the Spirit. I love our God and He never ceases to amaze me. Here is her testimony in her words.

Testimony

I prayed to God concerning a renewed mind towards losing weight, and God answered my petitions. I begin working out three to four days weekly, and God helped me walk up to three miles. I began to feel so much better. Towards the ends of September, right before being blessed with a new job, I was walking down the hallway in my home, and my knee popped very loudly. I screamed out in pain so loudly that I woke my son up, and he had to help me to my bed.

I somehow injured myself so bad that I could not raise my right leg off the floor. I started icing my knee, treating it with Epsom soaks, knee braces, and I began taking Ibuprofen in October to help with the internal swelling, all while praying for healing and anointing my knee with blessed oil.

I started my new job and I was working nine to ten hours a day (part time) and that did not help my situation due to working at a desk and not being able to really elevate it and give it the attention it needed.

Today after dealing with this issue for almost two months, I called for prayer, realizing the only way this situation would change was by calling on the name of Jesus. Elisha and I touched and agreed, and we commanded the pain, swelling and tightness to go! We also told my knee to be made whole. Whatever issues were there, be healed and align with the Word of God! Immediately I felt relief! No pain and minimal swelling, Elisha and I kept on praying. I felt the tightness start to fade! I started to test my knee out and after working almost ten hours today, I'm still pain free and there is no swelling. WHAT A MIGHTY GOD WE SERVE!

My "sister cousin," Sherlana. Michigan.

PRAYER AND ACTIVATION:

I love what God is doing in our families. Although we could not spend this Thanksgiving together due to COVID, I still thank God for all that He's doing. I can't imagine nor understand what most families are facing during this time, especially the ones who experienced loss this year. God wants us to know that He is love and wants His Divine Design for families. Some in the world over time have rejected His love and have fallen prey to Satan's traps. I was praying for families and wrote this prayer below. Stand in agreement with me for families. Let's talk to the Father together.

Dear Heavenly Father,

Thank You for this time of prayer together for families. We are extremely blessed because of it. We're thankful for Your hand that is on our families. We want Jesus to wash our bloodline, make it His own. The legacy and the heritage we have is laced with Your Holy Spirit and nothing else. It is only because of You that we've made it this far. Your hand is on our loved ones.
We each have a calling, a mandate, and we yield to You in every way. We give you praise for every prayer sent up to You by our ancestors, and we thank You for the matriarchs and the patriarchs. Those who were on the altar and those who found you later in life.
I know one day I will be looked on as someone who prayed for generations to come. So, I take a stand now and speak blessings over my children and my children's children. I pronounce over them a lifestyle of prayer and that miracles, signs, and wonders will follow them all the days of their lives. I bathe them in prayer now; they will sense Your presence with them,

they will believe Your report, and they will not be able to function unless they yield to You.

We just decree and declare that what You've already begun will continue even more within our families. Greater works shall we do because we choose to believe. We are proclaiming that we operate in our birthright. In Your Spirit of excellence, winning for Your Kingdom as every forerunner you've sent.

Everything that the enemy has tried to use against us, we cancel it now in the name of Jesus. Every day, we draw closer and experience manifestations of Your glory. We are living supernatural victorious lives, championing in You forever.

Thank You for every gift, and if any gifts are lying dormant, we speak a stirring up right now in the name of Jesus. That Your Holy Spirit will live in us, breathe in us, remember us, and all the prayers that have gone on before us. That we may be effective, efficient, and excellent in all that we do.

Lord, help us to remember that we are a part of Your government. In this world, but not of it. Our real home is heaven, and we are working in conglomerate with the heavenly angels. We speak signs, wonders, and miracles over our families. That we may be fruitful and productive. Great and glorious things are happening for our families.

Teach us to stay focused on Kingdom work, the Great Commission. We are in partnership and at work together with you Father. There are new dimensions and realms we are to see through You.

We decree and declare it now in Jesus' name. Amen.

Chapter Twelve

DECEMBER MIRACLES

"Heal the sick, raise the dead, cure those with leprosy, and cast out demons. Give as freely as you have received! Matthew 10:8

I'm still in awe of everything that God has done this year. I'm looking forward to all that God has planned. I'm so thirsty for the things of God. I'm going after His Kingdom realities, pursuing the greater works. Jesus has done so much for us. We can have new life now. We have access to the Father through Him. The Kingdom of Heaven is now in Jesus, and Jesus lives in us. Everyone can be transformed who receives Jesus. The only requirement is to yield to Him. It's free! Jesus paid the cost for us.

It hurt me to my heart when I received messages from people who asked what it would cost to schedule a prayer one-on-one session. I was troubled to learn that there are people today who require a payment before prophesying or praying for someone. I'm not at all against people giving offerings or tithing. That's a wonderful thing to do according to Malachi 3:10. But to charge someone who has nothing, that they may receive hope in return, is just wrong. Those people will have to answer to God.

Jesus gave the disciples the guide to follow when it comes to doing ministry. He said, "*...Give as freely as you have received.*" The heart that Jesus has is the heart that we should have. We can pray for the heart of Jesus and to love people from that place. Jesus gave to many His time and love, offering hope and adopting us into a new family of believers. I plan to continue sharing and giving freely. God has His ways of taking care of me. He doesn't need me to help Him do His job.

MONDAY, DECEMBER 5, 2020

During our Saturday Spirit Lifestyle session, I shared a testimony about a young lady who was having issues with her stomach, and the doctors were running several tests, but it was not clear what the issue was. I received a call to stand in agreement with her and another lady. I freely shared some scriptures and also shared some testimonies thinking the entire time how we can initiate healing through our faith by acting on God's Word. Sharing a testimony alone is sharing the testimony of Jesus and causes miracles.

One of the ladies and I took turns praying for the person with the stomach issues over the phone. While the lady was praying, I had a thought of a mother figure having the same issues. The thought just entered my mind. When this happens, I'm led to ask the person I'm praying for if it is true for them because it could be a word of knowledge revealed by the Holy Spirit. So, when the lady was done praying, I asked the person we prayed over if her mother had the same issues. She said, "Yes," and that her mom died from cancer also.

I felt that this daughter was being tormented, and it all had to do with her mother. She confirmed that she'd been dealing with anxiety and depression ever since her mom died. She had been carrying the pain of her loss. It has been a hard time for her. If this pain and sorrow resonates with you, consider praying the prayer at the end of this chapter. Consider renouncing, disallowing, and dispossessing all the heavy spiritual stuff you've been carrying.

After prayer, the lady started feeling so much better after that. Days later, she was still well and had to remind herself to stay away from those thoughts. To reject those lies that she would die also with the same ailments that her mother suffered from. It is a challenge to do that, but if we come into agreement with grief or the thoughts and feelings that lead to anxiety and depression, it will overtake us. It is a spiritual and mental sickness that needs to be addressed so that physical healing can manifest. She agreed to let God into those difficult places and commit to a Holy Spirit lifestyle that would hold her accountable.

If you or someone you know is praying to be free, pray to the Lord to show all the heavy bricks that are capping off the well of the Spirit from flowing. Make this a part of everyday prayer. We need to be free ourselves, and we can help lead others to the truth of God's love and purpose. We can ask for prophesy and words of knowledge also.

I never thought God would reveal secrets to me until I read 1 Corinthians 14, but as I prayed according to the Word of God and not the way I thought, He started to drop things in my spirit. Like knowing the mother of the woman with the stomach issues suffered in like manner. There's no way I could have known that with my own knowledge. It is His love and compassion for us and for those we pray for. And the more we pray, the more we are exposed to how He speaks and operates. Not praying limits our exposure. Not spending enough time in His presence will keep us from experiencing all the wonderful possibilities that come with our relationship with the Father.

Sin also shields us from His glory. Sin, shame, and guilt do not mix with the glory of God. We can get rid of all of it! It is possible! He's worth it. Life with Him is the only way to function and be completely free.

MONDAY, DECEMBER 12, 2020

My friend Darchal called with concerns for her mother. Her mother was giving up on life. She had been suffering from depression for as long as she could remember. This year, she went over the edge and it took a turn for the worse. Darchal was crying and admitted to having depressing thoughts and crying spells herself. She needed her mom well and felt like her mom was giving up hope. Something important that she told me was that whenever things would go wrong in her life, she would just want to throw in the towel. She was angry at Satan, but at the same time, would verbally say, "Bring it on. It is what it is. What's next?"

I told her that's a mistake, that she came into agreement with the oppression, like opening the door to the devil. She repented and renounced those words she spoke over herself, that she will never give up again. We started to pray for her first, for her to be free from the heaviness that was oppressing her. For her to lay down this whole year and give it to Jesus. It was an interesting experience. While praying for her, I felt something float up off my head, like a heavy metal band was pulled upward—more like snatched upward from my head. When things like this happen during prayer, I take it as a word of knowledge of the manifestations that could be happening for the person I'm praying for. I asked her if she was feeling anything. She said she felt something come off, something left her. Hallelujah! I thank the Holy Spirit for that confirmation. She was speaking differently after our prayer and was ready to pray for her mother.

Her mother was in the hospital because her body began to shut down from not eating. They could not do anything to get her to respond. They were considering hospice care, not COVID-related. But no one could get in the hospital because of COVID restrictions—no visitors whatsoever. So, I recorded a prayer and told her the next opportunity she got, to play this prayer for her mother. We prayed against the spirit of oppression and depression, that God would deliver her.

Darchal was encouraged but was wondering how she would get to her mom. I encouraged her that God is already there, and we prayed for the angels of the Lord to be on guard in her mom's hospital room.

She told me that they are not allowing family in the hospital because of COVID restrictions. I prayed that the doors would open for her soon, that she would be allowed in to reach her mother.

We ended our prayer call waiting and trusting God. Darchal did her regular routine calls and checks on her mom. While calling, she insisted on being let in so that she could pray for her mom. She called me back saying the hospital was letting her in suddenly. Hallelujah! God answers prayers.

I told her, just like God opened the door for her to get inside, watch what He is going to do for her mother. I didn't know what and how God would do it, but I spoke what I felt in my heart. Breakthrough was coming. She went inside and immediately played the prayer for her mother. Her mother was still not eating, talking, or responding. It looked bad. But Darchal waited on God and slowly things started to happen.

She said she saw her mom being transformed before her very eyes. She started responding slowly and eventually doing everything that she was not doing before—things that she couldn't do before. This was just simply amazing. I'm so happy she got her mom back. God gets the glory. Here's the testimony from Darchal; these are her words.

Testimony

I called to ask for prayer for my mother, and I saw her being transformed before my eyes. She was in the hospital; doctors basically couldn't find anything wrong with her. They wanted to put her in hospice because she was shutting down. She was plagued with depression and other entities. I could only see her on Facetime because of COVID restrictions. When we prayed, you told me to play a recorded prayer for her. That same day, the hospitals let me in to see my mother. Now my mom is home and doing much better. I'm grateful. Thanking God for working through you, Elisha, and Dameon Brown.

Darchal and her mother. Michigan.

WEDNESDAY, DECEMBER 16, 2020

I can't possibly speak for everyone, but I know there are a few people that at some time or another, dealt with the same thoughts I had. For the longest, I thought the worst of myself, focusing on my shortcomings, weaknesses, and mistakes. Over time, I allowed God to heal me from that toxic way of thinking. I learned that what we see as weaknesses, God sees as mighty. The heart is what God sees (1 Samuel 16:7). He doesn't care about the outward appearance, or what others may think. He desires to do amazing things in our lives, and it will happen if we don't fight against His process.

Jeremiah 29:11 says, "*For I know the plans I have for you, declares the Lord, plans for welfare and not for evil, to give you a future and a hope.*" So, when God puts us on someone's heart for a project, instead of running away from it, as I've been guilty of doing in the past, I take it and go forward in Jesus' name. Trusting He will take care of the details.

In Chapter 2, I mentioned modeling for a hotel and casino. I knew God led me there; it was obviously Him and how that entire opportunity fell on my lap. One of the other models/actors was Roxanne Steele. Roxanne is an accomplished radio host, producer, and social blogger. She did all the voiceovers for the commercial. What I didn't know at the time was that she was one of the hosts for the "New Country 93.1" FM radio station. One of the #1 stations in our city! She had this life I didn't see or know about. And I was a Spirit Lifestyle Coach, which she didn't know about.

We exchanged contact information back in February and kept in touch online. God touched her heart to create "Prayer Request Wednesday." It was an hour where people could submit prayer requests through calling in, email or text. They would try to share encouraging words and have someone on to pray at the end of the hour to seal our agreement as we stood in faith for the city, the region, and the world.

Roxanne messaged me asking if I would be their featured guest on the radio show to offer prayers. Old Elisha would ask questions like, "Why me?" There's, like, *millions* of preachers everywhere who could pray on the station. But I didn't blink. I said I would do it. I didn't know it would turn into a weekly thing. But it did. They loved the prayers and invited me to be a part of their efforts every week.

Very traditional people would probably say, "But it's not a Christian station." I only think about Jesus and how, if He were here, He would not spend most of His time hanging out in churches every day, He'd be where the people are. I would not have met Roxanne if I turned down the casino modeling opportunity worrying about what people would say. I'm glad I listened to God and followed His plans, which were for me to begin speaking His name every Wednesday on the country music station. People from all different beliefs were listening in and calling into the station. Atheists, Muslims, Agnostics, Christians, etc. Anyone who loved country music. They asked me to pray a generic prayer. I didn't know how it would be received, but I represent Jesus no matter where I go. And if He put me on their hearts, I can only imagine it's because He wants me to shine His light. I ended each prayer, "In Jesus' name."

Listeners were calling in for prayers for cancer, infertility, multiple sclerosis, depression, anxiety, etc. I know that not everyone knew Jesus, but I prayed with all my heart that everyone under the sound of my voice would get to know Him.

Seeds are sown, and they are reaching places I can only dream about. If I'm on the station, I will proclaim the excellences of Him who called me out of darkness into His marvelous light (1 Peter 2:9). I intercede for our nation, our cities, our regions, and the world. That we will find Him, turn from evil, pray and be healed. Second Chronicles 7:14 says, "*If my people, which are called by my name, shall humble themselves, and pray, and seek my face, and turn from their wicked ways; then will I hear from heaven, and will forgive their sin, and will heal their land.*" It's an honor to be a witness to the Kingdom of God, to work to build what's important to God. To be His ambassador. This entire year has been an open display of what I have been doing in secret for so many years. It really blows my mind. God gets the glory.

THURSDAY, DECEMBER 24, 2020

HEALING FOR CHRISTMAS

I received a message from one of my uncles saying that my aunt wasn't feeling well. His message came in right when I was praying, so I continued in prayer for my family. I asked our Holy Spirit what the source of this issue could be. I heard "pressure."

I continued praying and asked God "Pressure where?"

I then heard "lower back." I prayed that God would move that issue in the name of Jesus. Then I called my aunt. Although she's my auntie, she's also my godmother. So, I often call her "auntie mommy." She's the one who goes out of her way for everybody. She coordinated my entire wedding and handmade all my bridesmaids' dresses. She went with me for my wedding dress fitting. I just have so many good memories with her, and I know so many others do also.

I spent a lot of time with her as a baby. She would keep me sometimes and care for me. She was instrumental in my life then even before I knew it and now as an adult. I called her over the phone, and she shared with me what had been going on. She told me that she'd been in pain for a week. She confirmed that it was her back indeed that was the issue.

The Holy Spirit revealed it beforehand, and I believe it was because she was soon to be healed. I've noticed a pattern all year, God reveals to heal. She told me she'd been using support for her back and was having trouble sleeping; the pain would wake her up at night, and it was nonstop. This is very unusual and not something she had to deal with before. I figured it was a spiritual attack on her and my uncle. They both do ministry, and God uses them to touch others. Satan doesn't like that. She's a powerful evangelist and holds various titles in her denomination. In fact, when I called her, she was wrapping up another call where she was praying for someone else. Can you picture her now? I thought to myself, wow, giving of her time and love, just like Jesus did, even though she was not feeling her best. How many times has someone continued to do ministry when they weren't feeling well themselves? It doesn't matter the curve balls the enemy tries to send her way, she's not going to give up! She contends and believes for herself and others. I know because she believed for me. I learn so much from my conversations with her. She reminds me so much of my grandmother (the late Mo Nellie Upshaw). I can see grandma in all my aunties.

I asked my aunt to rate her level of pain while we were talking. She said it was an eight out of ten (ten being the worst pain). We just stood on the Word of God together over the phone. We prayed scriptures that I normally pray in all cases, like Mark 11:25, Psalms 103:2-3, and Joel 2:32. She noticed that the pain dropped to a level two. It always works like that, the moment we get scriptural stuff that's to happen. We were excited and rejoicing and kept praying. She started to pace around her room without the support that she was using, all while giving God praise. We both were just thanking and worshiping Him. He is so good, all the time!

I checked on her the next day, and she was still praising God. She had a great night! Zero pain and slept wonderfully. That's our Jesus!! She's moving freely again and completely received her healing through Jesus. What she prayed about for others; God did for her—so awesome. Now she can enjoy Christmas and more time with family, yay! A miracle for Christmas! What a beautiful gift I thought. Miracles are happening daily, and now this, so close to Christmas. The day we set aside to acknowledge Jesus being born into this world, to save us and do exactly this: heal, deliver, and set free.

My Auntie Mommy Vanessa. Michigan.

WEDNESDAY, DECEMBER 30, 2020

NEW YEAR'S EVE MIRACLE

It is New Year's Eve. I received a message from a lady named Paula who was suffering from severe hip pain. This was our first time speaking. She saw a testimony that I shared online and thought she'd reach out in hopes of receiving prayer. I responded to the message, and we scheduled a time to talk over Messenger. I called her, and she sounded so heavy over the phone, so I planned not to keep her long. She told me that she was encouraged by the testimonies that I shared. That it is mind-blowing to know that things like that are happening today. I told her that this is the main reason I share testimonies. To get the word out that our Jesus loves us and wants us healed, and if we believe, miracles can happen again and again. We just have to trust Him and allow Him to do it His way.

I started to ask her about what she was experiencing in her body. She said she'd been suffering from severe hip pain, and it causes her to walk with a limp. She said her pain was at a level ten (ten being the worst pain). This explained the weariness I heard in her voice. I proceeded to ask her if she knew that Jesus wanted her to be healed. She said she didn't know Jesus, and she didn't know that He would want to heal her. So, I gave her some scriptures to explain: Romans 10:9, John 3:16,

Isaiah 9:6-7, and 1 John 2:2. I asked her if she could believe in Jesus. She said, "Yes," and gave her life to Him right in that moment.

Next, we started to repent for all the sins and things that she was carrying from before giving her life to Jesus. I told her how wonderful it is now that she's covered by the blood of Jesus according to Isaiah 53:5. We shared on Matthew 18:18-20, Mark 11:25, Psalms 103:2-3, and Joel 2:32. We prayed these scriptures while giving God the glory.

I then commanded the pain in her hip to leave and report to the feet of Jesus. Believing that the Holy Spirit would flush all of it out and occupy that place where that pain used to be. That Jesus would move all abnormalities in her muscular system, skeletal system, and nervous system, praying for healing to flow from the crown of her head to the soles of her feet. To prove Himself to her, this daughter who just gave her life to Him. Just like He healed her soul from sin, He is the healer for her body, freeing her from pain and sicknesses.

I asked her to test it out to see if there were any changes. She was very quiet for a moment, but then said, "Oh, my goodness! Oh, my goodness! I'm walking without a limp!"

I told her that He's with her, and He's real. That's just like our Jesus. He loves her, and it is not His desire for her to be in pain. I asked her about the pain level, and she started searching for it. She said she could hardly find it, that maybe it dropped to a "one." We laughed, rejoicing, and praising God. I can tell she was quite shocked how God addressed her case so quickly.

Moments like these remind me of the time I had my first encounter with the Holy Spirit. Jesus was so real, and I knew my life would never be the same from that moment. We prayed again for all remaining pain to leave and never to return. We ended our conversation rejoicing and in tears. I don't know if we will ever cross paths in person, but we shared this glorious moment together in the Spirit as family. I spoke with her briefly later through texting. She is still doing well and so thankful for all that God has done. I'm so excited for her to have given her life to Jesus and receive healing before entering another year. Next year will be different for her. Old things are passed away and behold all things become new (2 Corinthians 5:17). Glory to Jesus forever! Miracles Are Activated by Someone Who Believes.

What a year it has been for miracles!

PRAYER AND ACTIVATION:

God has done so many awesome things, even though some were in the middle of a pandemic. Many things I didn't have the chance to document. But what I have I release so the world could know that our God saves, heals, and delivers. If we focus on any other source, we run the risk of falling victim to deception. This is my prayer:

Dear Heavenly Father,

Thank You for covering Your people. You comfort and strengthen those who are devastated by loss or recovering from epidemics and pandemics. Touch those who are feeling the financial restraints, challenges in marriages, just overall discouragement. Deliver those who are emotionally drained, dealing with anxiety and depression. Cause everyone to live in a place of devotion within themselves, not just in the four walls of a church building. Move your people from tradition to relationship with You.
Thank You for the strength to look up, to know that heaven and earth shall pass away, according to Matthew 24:35, but Jesus will never fail. Your Word will always stand true. No matter how hard it gets, no matter the challenge, teach us how to pray about everything and have peace of mind. We function in love and gentleness. You see our tears, and You hold our hearts in Your capable hands. We love You and want to make You smile according to Proverbs 16:15, "When the king smiles, there is life; his favor refreshes like a spring rain." We decree and declare that we live in this place and benefit from your rain.
Whatever the next years bring, our hearts say "Yes, Lord," and we remain yielded. We completely decrease so that you may increase in power. That your divine intelligence and the new covenant through Jesus

is implemented in us. We give you total rights as we lay our lives at your feet. If there is anything that is not in your plans, we thank you that those things are dissolved and dissipated. Give us a heart positioned for hope. To never give up no matter the circumstances, that miracles will continue to happen. We declare that we will all stay in expectation according to Romans 15:13, "*I pray that God, the source of hope, will fill you completely with joy and peace because you trust in him. Then you will overflow with confident hope through the power of the Holy Spirit.*"
2 Corinthians 13:14, "*May the grace of the Lord Jesus Christ, the love of God, and the fellowship of the Holy Spirit be with you all.*"
Numbers 6:24-26, "'*May the Lord bless you and protect you. May the Lord smile on you and be gracious to you. May the Lord show you his favor and give you his peace.*"
In Jesus' name, amen and amen.

SPECIAL THANKS

I'm so thankful to our heavenly God, our Jesus and beloved Holy Spirit, for teaching me and giving me the grace to share openly these testimonies. Thanks to my husband and best friend Dameon Brown Sr. for covering, encouraging, and speaking into me and our children Salah, Dameon Jr. and Elisha. I'm so blessed to have a family that understands me and loves working to build the Kingdom of God as much as I do. Thanks for your patience as we've taken the steps to do ministry on a global scale. I also appreciate my parents, aunt's, uncles, cousins, everyone for believing with me, for encouraging me to be bold and do what God placed in my heart to do.

Thanks to Rob and Aliss Cresswell for being trailblazers and encouraging me to become a coach! Thanks for partnering with me and mentoring me on this journey.

Thanks to Romany Tyrrell for encouraging me to write down all my experiences. She told me that I would probably write a book one day. I never saw it coming, yet here I am.

Thanks to Claire Kay for coaching me, sharing prophetic words and encouragement.

Thanks to all of Spirit Lifestyle staff and coaches. It has been an amazing adventure.

Thanks to Pastor Mark Yow for encouragement, mentorship, and prophetic words.

Thanks to Pastor Ben and Agnes Odongo for the prayers and prophetic words.

Thanks to my Pastors, Jerry & Joy Weinzierl for encouraging me with Joshua 1, equipping and teaching to be bold and courageous, to step out in faith to serve community and transform hearts for Jesus.

Thanks to every person who has shared sessions with my husband and I, whether over Zoom or in person.

Big thanks to every person who has consented to share their testimonies to promote the delivering and healing power of Jesus. I love you, and I thank the Lord daily for what He's doing in and through us all!

What an amazing journey it has been. I'm so excited for all that's to come with our Beloved Holy Spirit.

Milton Keynes UK
Ingram Content Group UK Ltd.
UKHW020935160924
448404UK00014B/868

9 798986 280707